Bernhard Pick

Luther as a Hymnist

Bernhard Pick

Luther as a Hymnist

ISBN/EAN: 9783337127206

Printed in Europe, USA, Canada, Australia, Japan

Cover: Foto ©ninafisch / pixelio.de

More available books at **www.hansebooks.com**

LUTHER

AS

A HYMNIST.

BY

REV. BERNHARD PICK.

PHILADELPHIA:
LUTHERAN BOOK STORE.
1875.

Entered according to Act of Congress, in the year 1875

By G. W. FREDERICK,

In the Office of the Librarian of Congress, at Washington, D. C.

Dedicated

TO

THE MEMORY OF HIM

WHO

"BY HIS SONGS HAS DONE MORE HARM TO THE ROMANISTS THAN BY HIS SERMONS."

PREFACE.

THE little volume which we offer to all Evangelical Christians is a compilation from various sources. This work of compilation has been a labor of love, the recreation of leisure hours from graver duties. Luther's songs are history, and the history of the Reformation cannot be understood without them. Says Mr. Coleridge: "Luther did as much for the Reformation by his hymns as by his translation of the Bible. In Germany the hymns are known by heart by every peasant; they advise, they argue from the hymns, and every soul in the church praises God, like a Christian, with words which are natural and yet sacred to his mind." And a modern writer remarks: "These hymns made a bond of union among men who knew little of Creeds and Articles. While theologians were disputing about niceties of doctrine, every devout man could understand the blessedness of singing God's praises in good honest German, instead of gazing idly at the Mass, or listening to a Latin litany. The children learned Luther's hymns in the cottage, and martyrs sang them on the scaffold."

Where some historical facts are connected with a hymn a few words have been said. Some hymns, which are best known, we have given in more than one version, especially the "Hymn of the Reformation," which will be found in *sixteen* different versions. With regard to this hymn we will also state that there is a *Hebrew* translation of the same, in a collection of hymns translated from the German and English into Hebrew, entitled, "Songs of Zion," for the use of the Hebrew Christians at Jerusalem and London.

The sources whence the translations for this collection have been drawn are given under the heading of each hymn. In the arrangement we followed the order of the Christian Year.

And now go forth, thou little book, and show the Christians how Luther believed, prayed, and sang; for

"False masters now abound, whose songs indite;
Beware of them, and learn to judge them right:
Where God builds up His Church and Word, hard by
Satan is found with murder and a lie."
(Luther.)

B. PICK.

ROCHESTER, N. Y.

CONTENTS.

	PAGE
PREFACE,	5
BIOGRAPHICAL SKETCH,	9
ADVENT,	31
Nun komm der Heiden Heiland (two versions),	31–35
CHRISTMAS,	36
Vom Himmel hoch da komm ich her,	36
Vom Himmel kam der Engel Schaar,	39
Christum wir sollen loben schon,	41
Gelobet seist du, Jesu Christ (two versions),	42–46
EPIPHANY,	47
Was fürcht'st du Feind Herodes sehr,	47
EASTER,	49
Jesus Christus unser Heiland der den Tod,	49
Christ lag in Todesbanden (two versions),	50–55
WHITSUNTIDE,	56
Komm Heiliger Geist, Herre Gott (six versions),	56–66
Komm Gott, Schoepfer, Heiliger Geist,	67
Nun bitten wir den Heiligen Geist,	70
THE TRINITY,	73
Der du bist drei in Einigkeit,	73
Gott der Vater wohn uns bei (two versions),	74, 75
A SONG CONCERNING THE HOLY CHRISTIAN CHURCH,	76
Sie ist mir lieb die werthe Magd,	76
THE TRIUMPH OF FAITH,	78
Ein feste Burg ist unser Gott (sixteen versions),	78–106
THE CHURCH,	107
Es spricht der Unweisen Mund (two versions),	107–110
Ach Gott vom Himmel sieh darein (two versions),	111–114
Wär' Gott nicht mit uns diese Zeit,	115

	PAGE
GRACE,	116
Nun freut euch, lieben Christen g'mein (two versions),	116
Wohl dem, der in Gottesfurcht steht,	122
Es wolt uns Gott genædig sein,	124
LAW,	126
Mensch willt du leben seliglich,	126
Diess sind die heiligen zehn Gebot,	127
THE CREED,	131
Wir glauben all an einen Gott,	131
THE LORD'S PRAYER,	133
Vater unser im Himmelreich (two versions),	133–138
PRAYER,	139
Verleih uns Frieden gnædiglich,	139
BAPTISM,	140
Christ unser Herr zum Jordan ging,	140
REPENTANCE,	144
Aus tiefer Noth schrei ich zu dir (four versions),	144–150
THE LORD'S SUPPER,	151
Jesus Christus, unser Heiland der von uns,	151
Gott sei gelobet und gebenedeiet,	153
DEATH,	156
Mitten wir im Leben sind,	156
Mit Fried und Freud fahr ich dahin,	159
PRAISE,	161
Jesaja, dem Propheten, das geschah,	161
THE TE DEUM,	162
Herr Gott, dich loben wir,	162
MISCELLANEOUS,	166
Erhalt uns Herr, bei deinem Wort,	166
Nun treiben wir den Pabst heraus,	167
Ein neues Lied wir heben an,	168
INDEX OF FIRST GERMAN LINES,	175
INDEX OF FIRST ENGLISH LINES,	177

BIOGRAPHICAL SKETCH.

"Iapeti de stirpe satum Doctore Luther
Majorem nobis nulla propago fuit."

DOCTOR MARTIN LUTHER, the bold and uncompromising Reformer, the Homer of Germany, was born at Eisleben, in Saxony, during a visit of his parents to that city, November 10th, 1483. His father, Hans Luther, a poor miner, who had previously resided in the village of Mohra, removed to Mansfeld the following year; and here it was that Martin received the first rudiments of education. At the age of fourteen he was sent to the Franciscan school at Magdeburg, where he used to sing in the streets for his bread, as his father was unable to support him. A year after, he went to Eisenach, and thence to the University of Erfurt, where, in 1503, he received his first degree, and two years later, having obtained the degree of

Doctor of Philosophy, he delivered lectures on the physics and ethics of Aristotle. Here, at Erfurt, it was that he for the first time found the Bible. His father had destined him to the study of the Law; but the impression produced on him by the fate of his friend Alexis, who was struck dead by lightning while walking by his side, on their road from Mansfeld to Erfurt, uniting with the effect of his early religious education, induced him to devote himself to the monastic life, and he entered the monastery of the Augustines in 1505, submitting patiently to all the penances which the superior of the order imposed upon novices. "Of a truth," he said, "I was a pious monk, and kept the rule of my order more strictly than I can tell. If ever a monk got to heaven by monkery, I was determined to get there. I strained myself to the very utmost, and tormented and plagued my body with fastings, vigils, prayers, and other exercises, far more than my bitterest enemies can torment me now. I, and others too, have toiled to the utmost, with a deadly sincerity, to bring our hearts and consciences to rest and peace before God, and yet could never find that same peace amid such horrible darkness." " For I knew Christ no more, save as a severe judge, from whom I sought to escape, and yet could not." In this distress of mind he was comforted by the Vicar-General Staupitz, who announced to him for the first time the great foundation-truth, that not in works and penance, but in "love toward God, and faith toward the Lord Jesus Christ," true repentance consists. " Seek not conversion in emaciation and suffering, but love Him who first loved thee."

From this time he was a zealous preacher and professor of theology. In 1510 he visited the court of Pope Leo X, at Rome. After his return, in 1512, he was made Doctor in Theology. In 1517 he published his " Theses," which, as Myconius, a contemporary, says, " flew over Germany as if the angels of God had been its messenger and carried them to all men's eyes." In 1518 Luther had a controversy with Dr. Eck, and the same year met the cardinal-legate Cajetan, at Augsburg. In 1520 came his open breach with the Pope, when he burnt the papal bull of excommunication, the " Bulla contra errores Martini Lutheri et sequacium."

In 1521 we see our hero at Worms, boldly confronting that august assemblage at the Diet. All eyes are centred upon the marvellous and intrepid monk, albeit slight traces of emotion are observed in his deportment, as he finds himself unsupported in the midst of so much pomp and pageantry of state; but soon he recovers his equanimity, all agitation subsides, and

> "There he stands in superhuman calm,
> Concentred and sublime! Around him pomp,
> And blaze imperial, haughty eyes, and words,
> Whose tones breathe tyranny, in vain attempt
> The heaven-born quiet of his soul to move;
> Crowned with the grace of everlasting Truth,
> A more than monarch among kings he stood!"
>
> (*Evenings with the Sacred Poets*, p. 90.)

Lucas Cranach's picture represents Luther as he stood there, so lone and strong, with his great fire-heart,—a new Prometheus, confronting the Jove of the sixteenth century and the German Olympus. "Here I stand; I cannot otherwise. God help me! Amen."

In 1522 we see Luther again at Wittenberg. In

1525 he married Catharine von Bora. Until the year 1546 he lived at Wittenberg, when he died on a journey, at Eisleben, at the age of sixty-three.

His great distinction of course lies in his great work of Reformation; but this subject does not come within the range of the present work. His poetical talent was shown in the department of sacred poetry. When, in 1526, a complete new German liturgy came out, and the want of German psalms and hymns in place of the Latin hymns and sequences was felt, Luther at once set to work to supply it.

He was intensely fond of both music and poetry, and was himself a master of vigorous and simple German. What he thought of music may be seen from what he said many years before Shakspeare wrote the famous passage about "the man that hath no music in himself:" "There is no doubt that many seeds of splendid virtues are to be found in such souls as are stirred by music; and them who have no feeling for it I hold no better than stocks and stones. If any man despises music, as all fanatics do, for him I have no liking; for music is a gift and grace of God, not an invention of men.

Thus it expels the Devil and makes people cheerful. Then one forgets all wrath, impurity, sycophancy, and other vices. Next to theology,"—*that* was with Luther the music of the spheres,—"I give music the highest and most honorable place; and every one knows how David and all saints have put their divine thoughts into verse, rhyme, and song." To his friend Spalatin he writes: "It is my intention, after the example of the prophets and the ancient fathers, to make German psalms for the people; that is, spiritual songs, whereby the Word of God may be kept alive among them by singing. We seek, therefore, everywhere for poets. Now, as you are such a master of the German tongue, and are so mighty and eloquent therein, I entreat you to join hands with us in this work, and to turn one of the psalms into a hymn, according to the pattern (*i. e.*, an attempt of my own) that I here send you. But I desire that all newfangled words from the Court should be left out; that the words may be all quite plain and common, such as the common people may understand, yet pure and skilfully handled; and next, that the meaning should be given clearly and graciously, according to the sense of the psalm itself." (Winkworth, Christ. Sing., p. 107, *seq.*)

Luther, besides writing some original hymns, translated a number of the grand old Latin hymns, which he counted among the good things that God's power and wonderful working had kept "alive amid so much corruption," and purified and adapted old German poems to the service of the temple. Thus the old ditty—

> "O thou naughty Judas!
> What hast thou done,
> To betray our Master,
> God's only Son!
> Therefore must thou suffer
> Hell's agony,
> Lucifer's companion
> Must forever be.
> Kyrie eleison!"

Luther changed to the following:

> "'Twas our great transgression
> And our sore misdeed
> Made the Lord our Saviour
> On the cross to bleed.

Not then on thee, poor Judas,
  Nor on that Jewish crew,
Our vengeance dare we visit,—
  We are to blame, not you.
    Kyrie eleison !

' All hail to thee, Christ Jesus,
  Who hungest on the tree,
And bor'st for our transgressions
  Both shame and agony.
Now beside thy Father
  Reignest thou on high ;—
Bless us all our lifetime,
  Take us when we die !
    Kyrie eleison !"

(Christ. Exam., 1860, p. 239, seq.)

Altogether Luther wrote about thirty-six hymns (more are frequently ascribed to him, but with doubtful accuracy), and which may be divided as follows :

(A.) TRANSLATIONS OF LATIN HYMNS.

1. Jesus Christus unser Heiland. From the Latin of John Huss : Jesus Christus nostra Salus.

BIOGRAPHICAL SKETCH. 17

2. Verleih uns Frieden gnädiglich. From the Latin Da, pacem domine (sixth or seventh century).
3. Christum wir sollen loben schon. From the Latin of Cölius Sedulus: A solis ortus cardine.
4. Der du bist drei in Einigkeit. From the Latin, O lux beata trinitas (fifth century).
5. Herr Gott, dich loben wir. From the Latin, Te Deum laudamus (fourth century).
6. Komm, Gott, Schöpfer, heil. Geist. From the Latin of Gregory the Great: Veni creator spiritus, mentes.
7. Komm, heiliger Geist, Herre Gott. From the Latin, Veni sancte spiritus, reple (fourteenth century).
8. Nun komm der Heiden Heiland. From the Latin of Ambrose: Veni redemptor gentium.
9. Was fürcht'st du Feind Herodes. From the Latin of Cölius Sedulus: Hostis Herodis impie.
10. Wir glauben All' an Einen Gott. From the Latin, Patrem credimus.

(B.) AMPLIFICATION OF GERMAN HYMNS FROM THE LATIN.

11. Gelobet seist du, Jesu Christ. From the Latin of Gregory the Great: Grates nunc omnes reddamus; to which he added six verses.
12. Mitten wir im Leben sind. From the Latin of Notker: Media vita in morte sumus: to which he added two verses.

(C.) CORRECTION AND REVISION OF GERMAN HYMNS.

13. Christ lag in Todesbanden. A revision and enlargement of the old "Christus ist uferstanden."
14. Gott der Vater, wohn uns bei. A correction of an old hymn of the fifteenth century.
15. Gott sei gelobet und gebenedeiet. A revision of a hymn of the sixteenth century, sung at high mass.
16. Nun bitten wir den heil. Geist. An enlargement of a hymn of the thirteenth century, to which he added three other verses.

(D.) HYMNS BASED UPON LATIN PSALMS.

17. Ach Gott vom Himmel sieh darein. Psalm 12: Salvum me fac domine.
18. Aus tiefer Noth schrei ich zu dir. Psalm 130: De profundis clamavi ad te.
19. Ein feste Burg ist unser Gott. Psalm 46: Deus noster refugium.
20. Es spricht der unweisen Mund. Psalm 14: Dixit insipiens in corde suo.
21. Es wollt uns Gott gnädig sein. Psalm 67: Deus misereatur nostri.
22. Wär' Gott nicht mit uns diese Zeit. Psalm 124: Nisi quia dominus.
23. Wohl dem, der in Gottesfurcht steht. Psalm 128: Beati omnes qui timent dominum.

(E.) HYMNS BASED UPON PASSAGES OF THE BIBLE.

24. Christ unser Herr zum Jordan kam. Matthew 3.
25. Diess sind die heiligen zehn Gebot. The Decalogue.
26. Jesaja, dem Propheten, das geschah. Isaiah 6.
27. Mensch willst du leben seliglich. The Decalogue.
28. Mit Fried und Freud ich fahr dahin. Luke 2.
29. Sie ist mir lieb, die werthe Magd. Revelation 12.
30. Vater unser im Himmelreich. Matthew 6.
31. Vom Himmel hoch, da komm ich her. Luke 2.

(F.) ORIGINAL HYMNS.

32. Ein neues Lied wir heben an.
33. Erhalt uns Herr, bei deinem Wort.
34. Jesus Christus, unser Heiland.
35. Nun freut euch, lieben Christen g'mein.
36. Vom Himmel kam der Engel Schaar.

These different hymns may be arranged in the following chronological order:

A.D. 1523. Nos. 17, 18, 32, 35.
" 1524. " 1, 3, 6, 7, 8, 10, 11, 12, 13, 14, 15, 16, 20, 21, 22, 23, 25, 27, 28, 34.
" 1526. " 26.
" 1529. " 2, 5, 19.
" 1535. " 29, 31.
" 1539. " 30.
" 1541. " 9 (Dec. 12), 24, 33.
" 1543. " 4, 36.

Luther's first hymn was, it is believed, called forth by the martyrdom of two young Christian monks, who were burned alive, at Brussels, by the Sophists, in 1523 :

" Flung to the heedless winds, or on the waters cast,
 Their ashes shall be watched, and gathered at the last;
 And, from that scattered dust, around us and abroad,
 Shall spring a plenteous seed of witnesses for God.
 Jesus hath now received their latest living breath,
 Yet vain is Satan's boast of victory in their death.
 Still, still, though dead, they speak, and, trumpet-tongued,
    proclaim
 To many a wakening land the one availing Name !"

These majestic stanzas, quoted in D'Aubigne's History of the Reformation, form indeed, in themselves and by themselves, though only a fragment, a sweet and soul-stirring poem. They speak to the heart like a trumpet. But it is not just the trumpet Luther blew. It is a little more silvery than that was. To change the figure, these lines (which are rather a transfusion than a translation) represent their original somewhat as do those ideal pictures of places painted after a lapse of time by artists of genius, and called *memories*. We can only hope to give, ourselves, a hint of the picture and the music; indeed, it seems impossible to combine in our modern speech the strong antique simplicity of the original, with its singular melody and harmony.

It was in the very autumn when Hans Sachs, who sat beating time on his lapstone to the music of the blessed revival, came forth with his " Nightingale,"—who, soaring above the clouds, announced the return of day to a world so long slumbering in darkness, or walking in a dim, dubious, malignant lunar light,—that Luther, hearing of the good confession the two Augustinian monks had witnessed at Brussels, sent forth his hymn with a letter to the churches in those parts, in the beginning of which he says that the word is fulfilled again: " The flowers appear on the earth, the time of the singing of birds is come, and the voice of the turtle is heard in the land."

The hymn, consisting of over a hundred lines, begins:

> " A brave new song aloud we sing,
>   To tell the wondrous story,
>   What God hath done, our Lord and King,
>   And sound his praise and glory.

"At Brussels, down in Netherland,
　The Lord of gifts and graces
Hath well revealed his mighty hand,
　By two young boys, whose faces
　Now shine in heavenly places."

Then, after detailing, in precisely this measure, the particulars of the trial, condemnation, and execution, it concludes with the stanzas which we referred to as having been so freely paraphrased, and which somewhat literally run as follows:

"Their ashes will not rest; world-wide
　They fly through every nation.
No cave nor grave, no turn nor tide,
　Can hide the abomination.
They whom the foe with murderous flame
　Had burnt to death,—upspringing,
Lo! in his ears they shout his shame,
　Till every land is ringing
　With their triumphant singing.

"Let Satan's lie go round;—'tis vain;
　Soon all his arts shall fail him;
God, in His Word, hath come again,—
　With thankful hearts we'll hail him.

> Hard by stands Summer at the door;
> Grim Winter's chain is broken;
> The tender flowers put forth once more:
> These things His hand betoken
> Who'll do what he hath spoken."

(*Christ. Exam.*, 1860, p. 243, *seq.*)

Luther's hymns, compared with Wesley's thousands, are rather small in number; "but they are to be weighed and not counted, and weighed, too, in the scales of an historian's and a Christian believer's living sympathy."

Spangenberg, in his Preface to the "Cithara Lutheri," in 1545, speaks thus of Luther's hymns: "One must certainly let this be true and remain true, that, among all Meister-singers, from the days of the Apostles until now, Lutherus is and always will be the best and most accomplished; in whose hymns and songs one does not find a vain or needless word. All flows and falls in the sweetest and neatest manner, full of spirit and doctrine, so that his every word gives outright a sermon of its own, or, at least, a singular reminiscence. There is nothing forced, nothing foisted in or patched up, nothing fragmentary. The rhymes are easy and good, the words choice and proper, the meaning clear and intelligible, the melodies lovely and hearty, and *in summâ* all is so rare and majestic, so full of pith and power, so cheering and comforting, that, in sooth, you will not find his equal, much less his master." (*Christ. Exam.*, p. 240.)

On the 18th of February, 1546, at 2 A.M., this hero ended his earthly career, and was buried in the castle church of Wittenberg. Over his grave his own great battle-hymn, "Ein feste Burg ist unser Gott," was sung amid sobs and tears.

Luther is represented as a man of low stature but handsome person, with a "clear, brave countenance," lively complexion, and falcon eyes. Antonio Varillas (Liber Hist. de Hæres) says: "Nature gave him an Italian head upon a German body; such was his vivacity and diligence, his cheerfulness and health." His voice was clear and penetrating, his eloquence overpowering. Melancthon, on beholding his picture, exclaimed, "*Fulmina erant singula verba tua.*" Another contemporary said of him, that he was a man "to stop the wrath of God." Another calls him the third Elias. He was a husband and a father, fond of society, of a free and jovial nature, much given to music, himself a composer and an able performer on the flute. A man of singular temperance and great industry. He throve best on hard work and spare diet. An easy life made him sick. As to his character, a man without guile, open, sincere, generous, obliging, patient, brave, devout. "He was not only the greatest," says Henry Heine, "but the most German man of our history. In his character all the faults and all the virtues of the Germans are combined on the largest scale. Then he had qualities which are very seldom found united, which we are accustomed to regard as irreconcilable antagonisms. He was, at the same time, a dreamy mystic and a practical man of action. His thoughts had not only wings but hands. He spoke and he acted. He was not only the tongue but the sword of his time. Moreover, he was at the same time a scholastic word-thresher and an inspired, God-intoxicated prophet. When he had plagued himself all day long with his dogmatic distinctions, in the evening he took his flute and gazed at the stars, dissolved in melody and devotion. He could scold like a fishwife, and he could be soft, too, as a tender maiden. Sometimes he was wild as the storm that uproots the oak, and then again he was gentle as the zephyr that dallies with the violet. He was full of the most awful reverence and of self-sacrifice in honor of the Holy Spirit. He could merge himself entirely in pure spirituality; and yet he was well acquainted with the glories of this world, and knew how to prize them; and out of his mouth blossomed the famous saying,—

"'Wer nicht liebt Wein, Weiber, und Gesang,
Der bleibt ein Narr sein Lebenlang.'*

"He was a complete man, I would say an absolute man, one in whom matter and spirit were not

---

* "Who loves not wine, and wife, and song,
Remains a fool his whole life long."

It may be true that this couplet has been framed out of the spirit and expressions of the great Reformer, and that in a rough and somewhat overstated manner they express certain qualities of his marked nature; but they are nowhere to be found in Luther's preserved writings, speeches, or divided. To call him a spiritualist, therefore, would be as great an error as to call him a sensualist. How shall I express it? He had something original, incomprehensible, miraculous, such as we find in all providential men,—something awfully *naive*, blunderingly wise, sublimely narrow; something invincible, demoniacal." (Hedge, *Prose Writers of Germany*.)

---

letters, and cannot be authenticated as from his lips. Some modern uses made of them are as untrue to his character and sentiments as they are to correct Christian morals. As Luther would have meant such words, had he used them, there is much truth, wisdom, and just humanity in them; but as some have taken them, under pretended authority of his name, they are thoroughly reprehensible and unchristian.—THE PUBLISHER.

A PREFACE TO ALL GOOD HYMN-BOOKS.

By Dr. Martin Luther, 1543.

Lady Musick speaketh.

Of all the joys that are on earth
Is none more dear nor higher worth,
Than what in my sweet songs is found
And instrument of various sound.
Where friends and comrades sing in tune,
All evil passions vanish soon;
Hate, anger, envy, cannot stay,
All gloom and heartache melt away;
The lust of wealth, the cares that cling,
Are all forgotten while we sing.
Freely we take our joy herein,
For this sweet pleasure is no sin,
But pleaseth God far more, we know,
Than any joys the world can show;
The Devil's work it doth impede,
And hinders many a deadly deed.
So fared it with King Saul of old;
When David struck his harp of gold,
So sweet and clear its tones rang out,
Saul's murderous thoughts were put to rout.

The heart grows still when I am heard,
And opens to God's Truth and Word;
So are we by Elisha taught,
Who on the harp the Spirit sought.
    The best time o' the year is mine,
When all the little birds combine
To sing until the earth and air
Are filled with sweet sounds everywhere;
And most the tender nightingale
Makes joyful every wood and dale,
Singing her love-song o'er and o'er,
For which we thank her evermore.
But yet more thanks are due from us
To the dear Lord who made her thus,
A singer apt to touch the heart,
Mistress of all my dearest art.
To God she sings by night and day,
Unwearied, praising Him alway;
Him I, too, laud in every song,
To whom all thanks and praise belong.

        (C. Winkworth, *Christian Singers*, p. 1.)

Advent.

Nun Komm der Heiden Heiland.

THIS hymn, which has been freely reproduced by Luther, is, as Dr. Schaff says, "the best of the Ambrosian hymns" (except the *Te Deum*, which is older), full of faith, rugged vigor, austere simplicity, and bold contrasts, but of objectionable taste in the third stanza, which is here smoothed down. St. Augustine, in his "Confessions," testifies to the effect of the hymns and music introduced into the church of Milan by Ambrose, his spiritual father. "How did I weep, O Lord! through thy hymns and canticles, touched to the quick by the voices of thy sweet-attuned church! The voices sank into mine ears, and the truths distilled into my heart, whence the affections of my devotions overflowed; tears ran down, and I rejoiced in them." The translation which we subjoin is from the Latin *Veni Redemptor gentium*, which is as happy as if it were a translation from the German.

(Schaff, "Christ in Song," p. 9.)

O THOU Redeemer of our race!
   Come, show the Virgin's Son to earth;
Let every age admire the grace;
   Worthy a God thy human birth!

'Twas by no mortal will or aid,
   But by the Holy Spirit's might,
That flesh the Word of God was made,
   A babe yet waiting for the light.

Spotless remains the Virgin's name,
   Although the Holy Child she bears;
And Virtue's banners round her flame,
   While God a temple so prepares.*

---

* Luther retaining the harsh features of the original—

    Alvus tumescit virginis,
    Claustra pudoris permanent,
    Vexilla virtutum micant,
    Versatur in templo Deus,

translates thus:
    Der jungfrau leib schwanger ward,
    Doch bleibt keuschheit rein bewahrt,
    Leucht' hervor manch tugend schon,
    Gott da war in seinem thron.

As if from Honor's royal hall
   Comes forth at length the Mighty One,
Whom Son of God and Man they call,
   Eager His destined course to run.

Forth from the Father's bosom sent,
   To Him returned, He claimed his own;
Down to the realms of death He went,
   Then rose to share the eternal throne.

An equal at the Father's side,
   Thou wear'st the trophy of Thy flesh;
In Thee our nature shall abide
   In strength complete, in beauty fresh.

With light divine Thy manger streams,
   That kindles darkness into day;
Dimmed by no light henceforth, its beams
   Shine through all time with changeless ray.

(J. C. Jacobi, "Psalmodia Germanica," I, p. 1.)

Now the Saviour comes indeed
Of the Virgin-Mother's seed,
To the wonder of mankind,
By the Lord himself designed.

Not begot like men unclean,
But without the stain of sin;
In our nature God was born
Us to save, who were forlorn.

Though the Virgin was with child,
Chastity proved undefiled;
All the female virtues here
Were inthroned, for God was there.

From His chambers forth He went,
Left the glorious element;
And like God and hero-man
He his blessed course began.

Coming from his Father's breast,
He returned to Him at last;
He, descending into hell,
Triumphed without parallel.

Thou who, Godlike every way,
Carry Thy victorious sway
In the flesh to such a length
That we gain Thy godly strength.

Lord, thy crib shines bright and clear,
Lightens night both far and near:
Let no darkness cloud this light,
That our faith be always bright.

Glory to the God of love!
Glory to His Son above!
Glory to the Holy Ghost!
Blessed Three, forever most.

Christmas.

Vom Himmel hoch da komm ich her.

A CHILD'S SONG AT CHRISTMAS CONCERNING THE LITTLE CHILD JESUS.

THIS carol Luther wrote for his little boy Hans, when the latter was five years old, and it is still sung from the dome of the Kreuzkirche in Dresden, before daybreak on the morning of Christmas Day. It refers to the custom then and long afterwards prevalent in Germany, of making at Christmas-time representations of the manger with the infant Jesus. Luther, however, abridged his original composition in 1543, and thus we find in most of the German hymn-books the abridged form, commencing, "Vom Himmel kam der Engel Schaar." The translation which we subjoin is the original form, as it was written by Luther for his son Hans.

(C. Winkworth, "Lyra Germ.," I, p. 12.)

FROM heaven above to earth I come,
To bear good news to every home;
Glad tidings of great joy I bring,
Whereof I now will say and sing.

To you, this night, is born a child
Of Mary, chosen mother mild;
This little child, of lowly birth,
Shall be the joy of all your earth.

'Tis Christ our God, who far on high
Hath heard your sad and bitter cry;
Himself will your salvation be,
Himself from sin will make you free.

He brings those blessings long ago
Prepared by God for all below;
Henceforth His kingdom open stands
To you, as to the angel bands.

These are the tokens ye shall mark,
The swaddling-clothes and manger dark;
There shall ye find the young child laid,
By whom the heavens and earth were made.

Now let us all, with gladsome cheer,
Follow the shepherds, and draw near
To see this wondrous gift of God,
Who hath His only Son bestowed.

Give heed, my heart, lift up thine eyes!
Who is it in yon manger lies?
Who is this child, so young and fair?
The blessed Christ-child lieth there!

Welcome to earth, thou noble Guest,
Through whom e'en wicked men are blest!
Thou com'st to share our misery,
What can we render, Lord, to Thee!

Ah, Lord, who hast created all,
How hast Thou made Thee weak and small,
That Thou must choose Thy infant bed
Where ass and ox but lately fed!

Were earth a thousand times as fair,
Beset with gold and jewels rare,
She yet were far too poor to be
A narrow cradle, Lord, for Thee.

For velvets soft and silken stuff
Thou hast but hay, and straw so rough,
Whereon, thou King, so rich and great,
As 'twere Thy heaven, art throned in state

Thus hath it pleased Thee to make plain
The truth to us poor fools and vain,
That this world's honor, wealth, and might,
Are nought and worthless in Thy sight.

Ah, dearest Jesus, holy Child,
Make Thee a bed, soft, undefiled,
Within my heart, that it may be
A quiet chamber kept for Thee.

My heart for very joy doth leap,
My lips no more can silence keep;
I too must sing with joyful tongue
That sweetest ancient cradle-song—

Glory to God in highest heaven,
Who unto man His Son hath given!
While angels sing with pious mirth
A glad New Year to all the earth.

Vom Himmel kam der Engel Schaar.

(Massie, "Spiritual Songs," p. 7.)

To shepherds, as they watched by night,
Appeared a troop of angels bright;
Behold the tender Babe, they said,
In yonder lowly manger laid.

At Bethlehem, in David's town,
As Micah did of old make known;
'Tis Jesus Christ, your Lord and King,
Who doth to all salvation bring.

Rejoice ye, then, that through His Son
God is with sinners now at one;
Made like yourselves of flesh and blood,
Your brother is th' eternal Good.

What harm can sin and death then do?
The true God now abides with you:
Let Hell and Satan chide and chafe,
God is your fellow—ye are safe.

Not one He will nor can forsake
Who Him his confidence doth make:
Let all his wiles the Tempter try,
You may his utmost powers defy.

You must prevail at last, for ye
Are now become God's family:
To God forever give ye praise,
Patient and cheerful all your days.

Christum wir sollen loben schon.

(From the Latin, "A solis ortus.") (Massie, "Spiritual Songs," p. 9.)

Now praise we Christ, the Holy One,
The spotless virgin Mary's Son,
Far as the blessed sun doth shine,
E'en to the world's remote confine.

He, who Himself all things did make,
A servant's form vouchsafed to take,
That He as man mankind might win,
And save His creatures from their sin.

The grace of God th' Almighty Lord
On the chaste mother was outpoured;
A virgin pure and undefiled
In wondrous wise conceived a child.

The holy maid became th' abode
And temple of the living God,
And she, who knew not man, was blest
With God's own Word made manifest.

The noble mother bare a Son,
For so did Gabriel's promise run,
Whom John confest and leapt with **joy**,
Ere yet the mother knew her boy.

In a rude manger, stretched on hay,
In poverty content He lay;
With milk was fed the Lord of all,
Who feeds the ravens when they call.

Th' angelic choir rejoice, and raise
Their voice to God in songs of praise;
To humble shepherds is proclaimed
The Shepherd, who the world hath framed.

Honor to Thee, O Christ, be paid,
Pure offspring of a holy maid,
With Father, Son, and Holy Ghost,
Till time in time's abyss be lost.

Gelobet seist du, Jesu Christ.

(Massie, "Spiritual Songs," p. 11.)

ALL praise to Jesus' hallowed name,
Who of virgin pure became
True man for us! The angels sing,
As the glad news to earth they bring,
    Hallelujah!

The everlasting Father's Son
For a manger leaves His throne;
The mighty God, th' eternal Good,
Hath clothed Himself in flesh and blood.
   Hallelujah!

He whom the world could not inwrap
Yonder lies in Mary's lap;
He is become an infant small,
Who by His might upholdeth all.
   Hallelujah!

Th' eternal Light, come down from heaven,
Hath to us new sunshine given;
It shineth in the midst of night,
And maketh us the sons of light.
   Hallelujah!

The Father's Son, God everblest,
In the world became a guest;
He leads us from this vale of tears,
And makes us in His kingdom heirs.
   Hallelujah!

He came to earth so mean and poor,
Man to pity and restore,
And make us rich in heaven above,
Equal with angels through His love.
    Hallelujah!

All this He did to show His grace
To our poor and sinful race;
For this let Christendom adore
And praise His nam for evermore.
    Hallelujah!

(J. C. Jacobi, " Psalmodia Germanica," I, p. 6.)

DUE praises to th' incarnate Love,
Manifested from above!
All men and angels now adore
What we nor they have seen before.
    Hallelujah!

The blessed Father's only Son
Chose a manger for His throne:
In this our nature's flesh and blood
Was clothed God the eternal Good.
    Hallelujah!

Who had the world at His command
Wants his mother's swaddling-band;
Th' Almighty Word vouchsafed to be
A little child like thee and me.
    Hallelujah!

Th' eternal Splendor shows His sight,
Gives the world its saving light,
And drives the clouds of sin away,
To make us children of the day.
    Hallelujah!

The Father's Son, by nature God,
Took amongst us His abode,
And opened through this world of strife
A way to everlasting life.
    Hallelujah!

In poverty He came on earth
To enrich us by His birth,
And make us heirs of endless bliss,
Like all the darling saints of his.
    Hallelujah!

All this was done that He might prove
What's the greatness of his love;
Which makes all Christians join to sing
Praise to our new-born God and King.
            Hallelujah!

Epiphany.

Was furcht'st du Feind Herodes sehr.

THIS hymn is from the Latin of Cœlius Sedulus,
"Hostis Herodes impie."

(Massie, "Spiritual Songs," p. 13.)

WHY, Herod, unrelenting foe,
Doth the Lord's coming move thee so?
He doth no earthly kingdom seek
Who brings His kingdom to the meek.

Led by the star, the wise men find
The Light that lightens all mankind;
The threefold presents which they bring
Declare him God, and Man, and King.

In Jordan's sacred waters stood
The meek and heavenly Lamb of God,
And He who did no sin, thereby
Cleansed us from all iniquity!

And now a miracle was done:
Six waterpots stood there of stone;
Christ spake the word with power divine,
The water reddened into wine.

All honor unto Christ be paid,
Pure offspring of the holy maid,
With Father and with Holy Ghost,
Till time in endless time be lost.

Easter.

Jesus Christus unser Heiland der den Tod.
(Massie, "Spiritual Songs," p. 15.)

JESUS CHRIST to-day is risen,
   And o'er Death triumphant reigns;
He has burst the grave's strong prison,
   Leading Sin herself in chains.
      Kyrie eleison.

For our sins the sinless Saviour
   Bare the heavy wrath of God;
Reconciling us, that favor
   Might be shown us through His blood.
      Kyrie eleison.

In His hands He hath forever
   Mercy, life, and sin, and death;
Christ his people can deliver,
   All who come to Him in faith.
      Kyrie eleison.

Christ lag in Todesbanden.

This hymn is based upon a Latin hymn of the fifteenth century, "Surrexit Christus hodie" (Daniel I, 341; and Wackernagel I, 175-177, who gives five forms); also upon an old Easter hymn, "Christ ist erstanden."

(C. Winkworth, "Lyra Germanica," I, p. 87.)

In the bonds of death He lay,
    Who for our offence was slain,
But the Lord is risen to-day,
    Christ has brought us life again;
Wherefore let us all rejoice,
Singing loud, with cheerful voice,
          Hallelujah!

Of the sons of men was none
    Who could break the bonds of death;
Sin this mischief dire had done,
    Innocent was none on earth;
Wherefore Death grew strong and bold,
Would all men in his prison hold,
          Hallelujah!

Jesus Christ, God's only Son,
    Came at last our foe to smite;
All our sins away hath done,
    Done away Death's power and right;
Only the form of Death is left,
Of his sting he is bereft,
             Hallelujah!

That was a wondrous war I trow,
    When Life and Death together fought;
But Life hath triumphed o'er his foe,
    Death is mocked and set at nought;
'Tis even as the Scripture saith,
Christ through death has conquered Death,
             Hallelujah!

The rightful paschal lamb is He,
    On whom alone we all must live,
Who to death upon the tree
    Himself in wondrous love did give.
Faith strikes His blood upon the door,
Death sees, and dares not harm us more:
             Hallelujah!

Let us keep high festival,
  On this most blessed day of days,
When God his mercy showed to all!
  Our Sun is risen with brightest rays,
And our dark hearts rejoice to see
Sin and night before Him flee:
          Hallelujah!

To the Supper of the Lord
  Gladly will we come to-day;
The word of peace is now restored,
  The old leaven is put away.
Christ will be our food alone,
Faith no life but His doth own:
          Hallelujah!

(J. C. Jacobi, "Psalmodia Germanica," I, p. 21.)

CHRIST was to death abased,
  And given for our transgression;
But by His being raised
  Regained us life's possession.

This should make our souls rejoice
To praise the Lord with heart and voice
In singing hallelujah.
    Hallelujah!

None yet was found of Adam's race
 Could conquer Hell and Devil;
Sin had defaced the former grace,
 None innocent, but evil;
Death was thus entailed on all,
Which got dominion by the fall,
 And kept us in his bondage.
    Hallelujah!

But Jesus, God's eternal Son,
 Is come for our salvation,
The cause of death He has undone,
 And stopped its devastation;
Ruined all his right and claim,
And left him nothing but the name,—
 His sting is lost forever.
    Hallelujah!

How strange and wondrous was this fray!
 Life was with Death surrounded;

The Lord of life here got the day,
   Death's kingdom was confounded.
This the Scripture doth record,
That Death was conquered with his sword,
   And led at last in triumph.
           Hallelujah!

Here is the very paschal Lamb
   By God himself appointed;
The prophets have foretold the same,
   That this was *the Anointed.*
With His blood our heart is signed,
No fear of death disturbs our mind,
   Subdued in that destroyer.
           Hallelujah!

This the day the Lord has made
   For our ejaculation;
Let heaven rejoice, let earth be glad,
   To praise His exaltation;
He dispels the clouds of sin,
His merit cleanses all within,
   We are removed from darkness.
           Hallelujah!

The bread of life we feed upon
  Is *Christ*, forever living;
The leaven of sin must be undone
  By grace, which He is giving;
Faith desires no other food
But our Redeemer's flesh and blood:
  Blest be His name forever!
    Hallelujah!

Whitsuntide.

Komm Heiliger Geist, Herre Gott.

THIS hymn has an abundant history of its own. Says Mr. Kübler (*Historical Notes to the Lyra Germanica*, London, 1865): "This is Luther's amplification of an old German version of the Latin Antiphona de Spiritu Sancto (*Veni Sancte Spiritus*). Luther added two verses to the one which he already found in use, and his hymn, with its old tune, was first published in 1524. It spread rapidly among the common people; in proof of which the fact may be adduced, that in the Peasants' War it was sung by the fanatical peasants at the bloody battle of Frankenhausen, in the year 1526; for when the Landgrave Philip of Hesse gave the signal for the attack against them, the peasants remained unmoved, neither retreating nor defending themselves, but waiting for the miraculous help of God, which their leader, Thomas Münzer, had predicted; they began to sing this pentecostal hymn, and continued singing until fifty thousand of them were slain and the rest dispersed.

"When Leonhard Kayser, on account of his Evangelical preaching, was burned alive in Passau on the 16th August, 1527, he asked the people to sing this hymn while he was tied to the stake. This they did, and when the flames rose high, he was heard several times to call, 'Jesu, I am thine; save me!'" And so he died. It has since often been used by ministers of the Gospel, not only in their preaching, but also on their dying beds. In many churches it was the standing hymn at the opening of divine service. A family in Silesia sang it during a fearful storm in 1535, when the roof of their house was blown away, but they themselves escaped without any injuries. The wife of the celebrated Frederic Perthes in Hamburg, the daughter of Matthias Claudius, wrote to her son, who was studying at the University, on his birthday: "My most earnest birthday wish and prayer for you is—

"'Thou strong Defence, thou holy Light,
Teach him to know our God aright,
And call him Father from the heart:
The Word of Life and Truth impart,
That he may love not doctrines strange,
Nor e'er to other teachers range;
But Jesus for his Master own,
And put his trust in Him alone.'

"My beloved child, may God fulfil this prayer to you!"

Luther's hymn first appeared in the *Erfurt Enchiridion* of 1524, where it has this title: "Here follows the hymn, *Veni Sancte Spiritus*, sung of the Holy Spirit, very useful and good." It was admitted into the Roman Catholic collection of M. Vehe, 1537.

FIRST VERSION.

Undoubtedly the first translations from German into English, as almost or quite the first hymnic provision in our language, were made by *Myles Coverdale* (1488?–1569), Bishop of Exeter in 1551, one of the earliest translators of the Bible, and a prominent Reformer. His *Goostly Psalmes and Spirituall Songes*, forty in number, appeared before 1539; a copy is preserved in the library of Queen's College, Oxford, and they are reprinted in his "Remains," published by the Parker Society in 1846. The first three are addressed "To the Holy Goost," and two of them are from Luther. "They are here given accurately," say the editors of the *Songs of the Spirit*, "even to the rude antique spelling, as memorials of a time when 'the rules of religion,' though 'strict,' were matters of fierce debate, but 'orthography was optional.'"

KOMM HEILIGER GEIST, HERRE GOTT. 59

Come, Holy Spirite, most blessed Lorde,
    Fulfyl our hartes nowe with Thy grace;
And make our myndes of one accorde,
    Kyndle them with love in every place
O Lorde, Thou forgevest our trespace,
    And callest the folke of every countre
To thy ryght fayth and truste of Thy grace,
    That they may geve thankes and synge to Thee.
             Alleluya, Alleluya!

O holy Lyght, moste principall,
    The Worde of Lyfe shewe unto us;
And cause us to knowe God over all
    For our owne Father moste gracious.
Lorde, kepe us from lernyng venymous,
    That we folowe no masters but Christe.
He is the Verite, His Worde sayth thus;
    Cause us to set in Hym our truste.
             Alleluya, Alleluya!

O holy Fyre, and comforth moste swete,
    Fyll our hertes with fayth and boldnesse,
To abyde by The in colde and hete,
    Contente to suffre for ryghteousnesse;

O Lord, geve strength to our weaknesse,
  And send us helpe every houre,
That we may overcome all wyckednesse,
  And brynge this olde Adam under Thy power.
    Alleluya, Alleluya!

SECOND VERSION.

From that rare and important volume, *Psalmodia Germanica,* or *The German Psalmody.* Translated *from the High German* by John Christian Jacobi, 1722. A supplement was added in 1725; the second edition, with supplement 1732, reprinted by *John Haberkorn* with a supplement of his own, 1760; the second edition of this, 1765. There is also a very rare reprint by Hugh Gaine, New York, 1756, "with which," says good Dr. Kunze, Lutheran pastor there in 1795, "many serious English persons have been greatly delighted." Jacobi was, indeed, except John Wesley, the only respectable translator from the German prior to our time; though far from a great poet, he is several steps above his Moravian successors. He rendered ninety-four hymns, and *Haberkorn,* who is inferior to him, thirty-three. Jacobi seems to have been Lutheran or Reformed rather than Moravian; but nothing is known about him.

Come, Holy Ghost! come, Lord our God!
Spread faith and love divine abroad,
And fill Thy longing people's minds
With precious gifts of sundry kinds.
O Lord, who by Thy heavenly light
Hast called Thy Church from sinful night,
Out of all nations, tribes, and tongues,
Thy praise shall make our choicest songs.
    Hallelujah! Hallelujah!

Thou Light of glory, gracious Lord!
Revive us by Thy holy Word,
And teach Thy flock in truth to call
On Thee, the Father of us all.
Delusive errors far remove,
And guide us always by that love
Which, keeping close to Jesus' path,
Rejects all other guides of faith.
    Hallelujah!

Thou great Dispenser of that love
Which sent Redemption from above,
O grant us faith and constancy
To conquer sin, and yield to Thee.

O Lord, by Thine almighty grace
Prepare us so to run our race
That we, from bonds of sin kept free,
May gain a blest eternity.
        Hallelujah!

THIRD VERSION.

From a collection of Psalms and Hymns published by him in 1851: an important book, made up largely of originals and translations from the German.

By Arthur Tozer Russel, then Vicar of Caxton.

BLEST Comforter, come, Lord our God,
And pour Thy gifts of grace abroad;
Thy faithful people fill with blessing,
Love's fire their hearts possessing.
O Lord, Thou by Thy heavenly light
Dost gather and in faith unite
Through all the world a holy nation,
To sing to Thee with exultation,
        Hallelujah! Hallelujah!

O holiest Light! Rock adored!
Give us Thy light, Thy living word,

To God himself our spirits leading,
With Him as children pleading.
From error, Lord, our souls defend,
That they on Christ alone attend;
In Him with faith unfeigned abiding,
In Him with all their might confiding.
        Hallelujah! Hallelujah!

O holiest Fire! Source of rest!
Grant that with joy and hope possest,
And in Thy service kept forever,
Naught us from Thee may sever.
Lord, may Thy power prepare each heart;
To our weak nature strength impart,
That we may, firmly here contending,
To Thee be daily hence ascending.
        Hallelujah! Hallelujah!

FOURTH VERSION.

By Miss Catharine Winkworth. From "Lyra Germanica," I, p. 117. Boston, 1864.

COME, Holy Spirit, God and Lord!
Be all Thy graces now outpoured
On the believer's mind and soul,
And touch our hearts with living coal.

Thy light this day shone forth so clear,
All tongues and nations gathered near
To learn that faith for which we bring
Glad praise to Thee, and loudly sing,
              Hallelujah! Hallelujah!

Thou strong Defence! Thou holy Light!
Teach us to know our God aright,
And call him Father from the heart;
The word of life and truth impart,
That we may love not doctrines strange,
Nor e'er to other teachers range,
But Jesus for our Master own,
And put our trust in Him alone.
              Hallelujah!

Thou sacred Ardor, Comfort sweet,
Help us to wait with ready feet
And willing heart at Thy command,
Nor trial fright us from Thy band.
Lord, make us ready with Thy powers;
Strengthen the flesh in weaker hours,
That as good warriors we may force
Through life and death to Thee our course!
              Hallelujah!

KOMM HEILIGER GEIST, HERRE GOTT. 65

FIFTH VERSION.

By Richard Massie, Esq. From Martin Luther's "Spiritual Songs."
London, 1854.

COME, Holy Ghost, Lord God, fulfil
With Thy rich grace, heart, mind and will,
And each believing soul inspire
With Thine own pure and holy fire.
Lord, by the brightness of Thy light,
Thou in the faith dost men unite
Of every land and every tongue;
This to Thy praise, O Lord, be sung,
   Hallelujah! Hallelujah!

Thou holy Light and Guide divine,
Oh cause the word of life to shine;
Teach us to know our God aright,
And call him Father with delight.
Keep us, O Lord, from all strange lore,
That we may seek no masters more,
But with true faith in Christ abide,
And heartily in Him confide.
   Hallelujah! Hallelujah!

Sweet source of comfort, holy Love,
Send us Thy succor from above,
That in Thy service we may stay,
And trouble drive us not away.
Lord, with Thy grace our souls refresh,
Confirm our frail and feeble flesh,
That we through life and death to Thee
May press with Christian chivalry.
    Hallelujah! Hallelujah!

SIXTH VERSION.

By Henry Mills. From "Horæ Germanicæ." New York, 1856.

Come, Holy Ghost, rule Thou within!
'Tis Thine by grace our souls to win;
Inspire with sacred joy the spirit
Of all who trust Thy word and fear it.
Thy light and truth hast Thou sent forth,
From east to west, from south to north,
To bring, from every tongue and nation,
A host to sing the great salvation.
    Hallelujah! Hallelujah!

Thou holy Light of truth divine,
From God's own word yet brighter shine,
That we thereby may better know Him,
And pay the love His children owe Him.
Thy teaching would we gladly learn,
And ever to another turn,
Our souls to Christ alone confiding,
In Him, who is our life, abiding.
    Hallelujah! Hallelujah!

Thou holy Portion, and our Rest,
Help us, that, with Thy comfort bless'd,
By troubles taught to prize thy favor,
We may rejoice in Thee forever!
By strength of Thine our weakness raise,
That, living, we may live Thy praise,
And, all the host of evil routing,
In death may triumph, fearless shouting—
    Hallelujah! Hallelujah!

Komm Gott, Schoepfer, Heiliger Geist.

THIS hymn is a translation of the old "Veni Creator Spiritus," the authorship of which is commonly attributed to Charlemagne, who died in the year 814.

Some ascribe it to St. Ambrose, the *Doctor Mellifluus et Mellitissimus* of the fourth century, while others would ascribe it to Gregory the Great, of the sixth century. But, says Mr. Benedict very truly (*The Hymn of Hildebert and other Mediæval Hymns*, New York, 1867), "except as a matter of literary history, it is of little importance who was the author. The merit of the hymn is in itself alone. Its comprehensiveness and brevity, its simplicity and beauty, its gentle spirit of trust and devotion, and its earnest directness of expression, mark it as the production of a great and practiced writer and a devout Christian, studiously familiar with the Scriptures and with theological truth, rather than of a proud monarch and a great soldier." Luther's rendering, which is tolerably close of the original, was admitted into the Romanist collection of Joh. Leisenritt, 1567. The version which we subjoin is by R. Massie, 1854.

> CREATOR, Spirit, holy Dove,
> Visit Thy people from above;
> Fill them with graces, and restore
> Thy creatures as they were before.
>
> For Comforter is Thy sweet name,
> A gift which from the Highest came,
> A ghostly Ointment from above,
> A living Fount, a fire of Love.

Our minds enlighten, and inspire
Our souls with love's celestial fire;
And since Thou know'st how frail we be,
Confirm and make us strong in Thee.

Thou, with Thy graces' sevenfold band,
The Finger* art on God's right hand;
Thou dost the Father's promise send
With tongues to earth's remotest end.

Drive far away our wily foe,
And by Thy grace sweet peace bestow;
That in Thy footsteps we may run,
And soul-destroying mischief shun.

Let us by Thee the Father know,
His Son, Christ Jesus, also show,
That, full of faith, we may know Thee,
Derived from both eternally.

---

* Trench, in his *Sacred Latin Poetry*, p. 184, says: "The title *digitus Dei* (finger of the Lord), so often given to the Holy Ghost, rests originally on a comparison of Luke 11 : 20, *si in digito Dei ejicio dæmonia*, with Matt. 12 : 28, *si autem ego in Spiritu Dei ejicio dæmonia*, where evidently the *digitus Dei* of Luke is equivalent to the *Spiritus Dei* of Matthew."

To God the Father, and the Son,
Who rose again, be honor done,
With Him, who came at Pentecost,
The Comforter, the Holy Ghost.

Nun bitten wir den Heiligen Geist.

This hymn was first printed in John Walther's Hymn-Book, 1524. The first verse is very old. A Franciscan monk, Berthold of Ratisbon, about A.D. 1250, in one of his sermons, gives the text of it, and exhorts his hearers to sing it often and heartily. That verse is attributed, says Miss Winkworth (*Christian Singers of Germany*, 1869), to Spervogel, a priest and favorite sacred poet of the twelfth century. Other verses, having some resemblance to Luther's, appeared in Romanist books a few years after the publication of his hymn, but there is no evidence that they are old. Luther's hymn was translated into Latin by Reinhart Lorich in 1550, and into Tamil by Ziegenbalg in 1723.

The hymn was once used under very peculiar circumstances, whereof the tale is told by Pastor Heiberg in his account of *Peter Palladius, the First Evangelical Bishop of Seeland:* see Karl Heinrich's *Erzählungen über Evang. Kirchenlieder.*

"In the earlier part of the sixteenth century, on the day preceding the festival of the Annunciation of the Virgin, about eighty fishermen were on the ice between Copenhagen and the island of Saltholm catching eels, when the ice gave way and broke up. They were carried along by the current, parted from each other, and in the end nearly thirty of them drowned. While they were still near together, one of them, Hans Vensen, who had been a pupil of Bishop Palladius, called out to the rest, 'Dear brethren, let us not fall into despair because we shall lose our lives; but let us prove by our conduct that we have been hearers of God's Word.' Whereupon they sang together *Nun bitten wir den Heiligen Geist*, and after it the hymn of the dying, *Mit Fried und Freud ich fahr dahin*, Luther's metrical version of *Nunc Dimittis*. When they had done singing, they fell on their knees, the water reaching their breasts, and prayed that God would grant them a happy death." (*Songs of the Spirit*, p. 236.) Our version is that by R. Massie, from Luther's *Spiritual Songs*, 1854.

Now crave we of the Holy Ghost,
What of all things we need the most,
True faith in Christ, when life is ending,
And from this grief we home be wending.
   Kyrie eleison.

Shine in our hearts, Thou worthy Light,
And teach us Christ to know aright;
Abiding in Thee, whose faithful hand
Hath brought us safe to our Fatherland.
     Kyrie eleison.

Grant us Thy favor, heavenly Dove,
And let us feel the glow of love,
That we may live with one another
As brother ought to live with brother.
     Kyrie eleison.

O Thou who hast so sweet a name,
Keep us from fear of death and shame,
Nor comfort in the hour refuse us
When Sin and Satan will accuse us.
     Kyrie eleison.

The Trinity.

Der du bist drei in Einigkeit.

(Mills, "Horæ Germanicæ," p. 223.)

Thou only God, the Three in One,
Eternal is Thy shining throne;
The Sun on us forbears to shine,
O cheer our souls with light divine!

At morn to Thee we offered praise,
With thanks our evening song we raise,—
For all Thy love would honor Thee
Now, onward, through eternity.

Our Father, praise to Thee we give;
Thou Son of God, our praise receive!
Thou Holy Ghost, we grace implore
To praise our God for evermore.

Gott der Vater wohn uns bei.

("Lyra Domestica," p. 111.)

Our God, our Father, with us stay,
And make us keep Thy narrow way;
Free us from sin and all its power;
Give us a joyful dying hour.
Deliver us from Satan's arts,
   And let us build our hopes on Thee,
Down in our very heart of hearts!
   O God, may we true servants be,
   And serve Thee ever perfectly.
Help us, with all Thy children here,
To fight and flee with holy fear;
Flee from temptation, and to fight
With Thine own weapons for the right.
   Amen, amen, so let it be!
   So shall we ever sing to Thee,
          Hallelujah!

Jesus Christ, be Thou our stay, etc., etc.

Holy Ghost, be Thou our stay, etc., etc.

(J. C. Jacobi, "Psalmodia Germanica," I, p. 27.)

God the Father, our Defence,
O save us from damnation;
All transgressions take from hence,
And grant us Thy salvation.
Guard us from the Tempter's snare
Within Thy own protection,
That under Thy direction
Our faith may 'scape infection.
We rely upon Thy care,
With all Thy well beloved
Thy grace be thus improved,
That we may ne'er be moved.
Amen, amen, be the word!
So shall we truly praise the Lord.

Lord Christ Jesus, our Defence,
O save us, etc., etc.

Blessed Spirit, our Defence,
O save us, etc., etc.

A Song

CONCERNING THE HOLY CHRISTIAN CHURCH.

Rev. 12 : 1-6.

Sie ist mir lieb die werthe Magd.

(R. Massie, "Spiritual Songs," p. 27.)

Dear is to me the holy Maid,—
I never can forget her;
For glorious things of her are said;
Than life I love her better:
    So dear and good,
    That if I should
    Afflicted be,
    It moves not me;
For she my soul will ravish
    With constancy and love's pure fire,
And with her bounty lavish
    Fulfil my heart's desire.

She wears a crown of purest gold,
  Twelve shining stars attend her;
Her raiment, glorious to behold,
  Surpasses far in splendor
      The sun at noon;
      Upon the moon
      She stands the Bride
      Of Him who died:
Sore travail is upon her;
  She bringeth forth a noble Son,
Whom all the world doth honor;
  She bows before His throne.

Thereat the Dragon raged, and stood
  With open mouth before her;
But vain was his attempt, for God
  His buckler broad threw o'er her.
      Up to His throne
      He caught His Son,
      But left the foe
      To rage below.
The mother, sore afflicted,
  Alone into the desert fled,
There by her God protected,
  By her true Father fed.

The Triumph of Faith.

Ein feste Burg ist unser Gott.

This is the most famous of Luther's hymns, founded on the forty-sixth Psalm, and which is supposed to have been written on his way to the Diet of Worms, from the coincidence of the third verse with Luther's answer to Spalatin, who tried to dissuade him from the journey: "If there were as many devils in Worms as there are tiles on the roofs, I would go, and would not be afraid. If Huss was burnt to ashes, the truth was not burnt with him." Some, however, think that it was composed at the close of the Second Diet of Spires—that in 1529, which revoked the religious liberty granted in the previous one of 1526. Be it as it is, this hymn of Luther has become the national hymn of Protestant Germany, the imperishable pæan of the Reformation, or as Heine called it, "the Marseillaise of the Reformation." Of the score or more of English versions of Luther's great hymn, we will give a few specimens.

FIRST VERSION.

From "Psalmodia Germanica," London, 1765.

God is our refuge in distress,
  Our strong defence and armor,
He 's present when we're comfortless,
  In storms He is our harbor.
    Th' infernal enemy,
    Look! how enraged is he!
    He now exerts his force
    To stop the Gospel course:
  Who can withstand this tyrant?

All human power is but dust,
  Our strength an idle story;
The *Valiant Man*, in whom we trust,
  Is Christ, the Lord of glory.
    He is the Conqueror,
    Vested with sovereign power.
    The Lord both great and good,
    The only living God,
  Gains us the field of battle.

If all the devils should wage the war
  In order to destroy us,

They should not once put us in fear;
The victory would be joyous.
   We dare the prince of hell;
   With fury let him swell;
   He cannot hurt one hair;
   We shall escape his snare;
Christ's single word can rout him.

His word puts all our foes to flight;
With shame they are confounded;
For Christ instructs our hands to fight;
His Spirit is unbounded.
   Tho' we should lose our lives,
   Fame, children, goods, and wives,
   Destroy hell what it can,
   'Twill find but little gain,
God's kingdom is our portion.

SECOND VERSION.

By Dr. W. L. Alexander, in "Lyra Christiana," Edinburgh, s. a.

A FORTRESS firm is God our Lord,
A sure defence and weapon;
Prompt help in need he doth afford
Let happen what may happen.

Our ancient wicked foe
Full of wrath doth go,
With much craft and might
In horrid armor dight:
On earth is not his fellow.

Of our own might we nothing can,
  We lie forlorn, dejected;
There fights for us the rightful Man,
  By God himself elected.
    Dost thou inquire his name?
    Jesus Christ? The same!
    Lord of hosts is He;
    Besides Him none can be:
'Tis He the field that keepeth.

And were this world of devils full,
  For our destruction eager,
That should not our firm faith annul;
  We would abide their leaguer.
    The prince of this lost world,
    From his empire hurled,
    Though with rage he roar,
    Is judged, and can no more;
A word shall overthrow him.

Hold fast that word which must remain,
  Let no dark doubt invade us;
He will be with us on the plain,
  With gifts and grace to aid us.
    Let life and honor fall,
    Let them take our all,
    Still our course we'll keep,
    No prize from us they'll reap;
  For us the kingdom waiteth.

THIRD VERSION.

By Bishop Whittingham, in "Hymns for Church and Home,"
Philadelphia, 1860.

A MOUNTAIN fastness is our God,
  On which our souls are planted;
And though the fierce foe rage abroad
  Our hearts are nothing daunted.
    What though he beset
    With weapon and net,
    Arrayed in death-strife?
    In God are help and life:
  He is our sword and armor.

By our own might we naught can do;
　　To trust it were sure losing;
For us must fight the right and true,
　　The man of God's own choosing.
　　　　Dost ask for his name?
　　　　Christ Jesus we claim;
　　　　The Lord God of hosts;
　　　　The only God;—vain boasts
　　Of others fall before Him.

What though the troops of Satan filled
　　The world with hostile forces?
E'en then our fears should all be stilled:
　　In God are our resources.
　　　　The world and its king
　　　　No terrors can bring;
　　　　Their threats are no worth;
　　　　Their doom is now gone forth;
　　A single word can quell them.

God's word through all shall have free sway
　　And ask no man's permission;
The Spirit and his gifts convey
　　Strength to defy perdition.

The body to kill,
Wife, children, at will,
The wicked have power,
Yet lasts it but an hour!
The kingdom 's ours forever!

FOURTH VERSION.

By Dr. W. M. Reynolds, in "Evenings with the Sacred Poets,"
New York, 1870.

A SAFE stronghold our God is still,
  A sure defence and weapon;
He will deliver from all ill
  That unto us can happen.
    Our old and bitter foe
    Is fain to work us woe;
    In strength and cunning, he
    Is armed full fearfully;
  On earth is not his equal.

By strength of ours we naught can do,
  The strife full soon were ended;
But for us fights the Champion true,
  By God himself commended.

And dost thou ask his name?
'Tis Jesus Christ! The same
Whom Lord of hosts we call,
God blessed over all—
He'll hold the field triumphant.

Tho' Satan's hosts the earth should fill,
All watching to devour us,
We tremble not, we fear no ill,
They cannot overpower us.
This world's false prince may still
Scowl fiercely as he will,
His threat'nings are but vain,
We shall unharmed remain;
A word shall overthrow him.

God's word unshaken shall remain,
Whatever foes invade us;
Christ standeth on the battle-plain,
With His own strength to aid us.
What tho' they take our life,
Our goods, fame, children, wife!
E'en when their worst is done
They have but little won,—
The kingdom ours abideth.

FIFTH VERSION.

By Thomas Carlyle, in "Critical and Miscellaneous Essays," vol. iii, New York, 1872.

A SAFE stronghold our God is still,
  A trusty shield and weapon;
He'll help us clear from all the ill
  That hath us now o'ertaken.
    The ancient prince of hell
    Hath risen with purpose fell;
    Strong mail of craft and power
    He weareth in this hour;
  On earth is not his fellow.

With force of arms we nothing can,
  Full soon were we downridden;
But for us fights the proper Man,
  Whom God himself hath bidden.
    Ask ye, who is this same?
    Christ Jesus is his name,
    The Lord Zebaoth's Son,
    He and no other one
  Shall conquer in the battle.

And were this world all devils o'er,
  And watching to devour us,

We lay it not to heart so sore,
  Not they can overpower us.
    And let the prince of ill
    Look grim as e'er he will,
    He harms us not a whit:
    For why? His doom is writ,
    A word shall quickly slay him.

God's word, for all their craft and force,
  One moment will not linger;
But spite of hell, shall have its course,
  'Tis written by His finger.
    And though they take our life,
    Goods, honor, children, wife,
    Yet is their profit small;
    These kings shall vanish all,
    The city of God remaineth.

SIXTH VERSION.

By H. W. Dulken, in "The Book of German Songs," London, 1871.

OUR God, a tower of strength is He,
  A good defence and weapon;
From every care He helps us free
  That unto us doth happen.

The old evil foe
With rage now doth glow;
Much cunning, great power,
His fearful armor are—
On earth there is none like him.

With our own might is nothing done;
We soon are lost and fallen;
There fights for us the righteous Man,
Whom God himself hath callen.
Dost ask who he is?
Christ Jesus, I wis;
The Lord Sabaoth,—
There is no other God,—
And He must be triumphant.

Though the world full of devils were,
All ready to devour us,
Still have we not such grievous fear,—
The victory is for us.
The prince of this earth
May scowl in his wrath;
But powerless must be,
For judgéd is he;
A word can overcome him.

His written Word shall they let stand,
And little thanks inherit;
He fighteth for us in the land
With His good gifts and Spirit.
And, take they the life,
Goods, fame, child, and wife,
Let all pass away;
Small profit have they;
The kingdom yet awaits us.

SEVENTH VERSION.

By H. Mills, in "Horæ Germanicæ," New York, 1856.

A TOWER of safety is our God,
His sword and shield defend us;
His mercy, too, relieves the load
Of evils that attend us.
But the ancient foe
Strives to work our woe;
Fearful power and art
In him their force exert;
On earth he has no rival.

By strength of ours naught could be done,—
  The strife full soon were ended;
But fights for us that righteous One
  By God himself commended.
    Needs his name be told?
    Jesus—from of old
    Lord of Sabaoth,—
    Our God and Saviour both,—
  He shall our souls deliver.

Though devils all the earth should fill,
  Each gaping to devour us,
This Saviour would our terrors quell,
  And victory guide before us.
    Prince of this vain world,
    Be thy fury hurled
    On our heads,—'twere vain!
    He will thy rage restrain;
  His smallest word subdue thee.

His truth our *foes* shall help to show;
  For this no thanks they merit;
Believing Him we onward go,
  He cheers us by His Spirit.

Should they, in the strife,
Quench our joys and life;
When their worst is done,
For us the victory's won,—
He'll crown us then with glory.

EIGHTH VERSION.

By Rev. R. P. Dunn, in "Sacred Lyrics from the German,"
Philadelphia, 1859.

A STRONGHOLD firm, a trusty shield,
When raging foes appal us,
Our God defence and help doth yield,
When heavy ills befall us.
With ancient bitter hate,
Such might and cunning great,
As guides no earthly arm,
Plotting us deadly harm,
Our foe attempts to inthral us.

Our human strength avails us naught,
Our struggles soon were ended,
And we in hellish snares were caught,
Unless by God befriended.

Know ye our Champion's name?
All heaven tells his fame,
" Jesus, the Lord of hosts."
His might our weakness boasts;
By Him are we defended.

What though in every path of life
  A host of fiends endeavor
To wound us in the deadly strife?
  Their arts shall triumph never.
    The author of all ill
    May threaten as he will;
    His throne and empire proud,
    But for a time allowed,
  A word shall end forever.

God's testimony standeth sure,
  Whatever man betideth,
He makes the weakest saint endure,
  Who in His grace confideth.
    Though the best gifts of life
    Our foes seize in the strife,
    We cheerful let them go;
    No profit have they so,
  For heaven ours abideth.

NINTH VERSION.

By N. L. Frothingham, in "The Monthly Religious Magazine,"
vol. xxxvii, Boston, 1867.

OUR God, he is a fortress-tower
   And armor to defend us;
In all this press of hostile power
   Deliverance He will send us.
     The old and wily foe
     Is bent to work us woe;
     With might and many wiles
     He smites and he beguiles;
   On earth there 's not his fellow.

With our own strength we nothing can,
   We soon sink down dejected;
There battles for us the right Man,
   Whom God himself elected.
     Ask who this can be?
     Jesus Christ is he;
     Lord Sabaoth his name,
     Which God alone can claim;
   He holds the field forever.

Though earth all full of devils were,
   All ramping to devour us,

We would not fear for their mad stir;
  They could not overpower us.
    The prince of this world,
    Grimmest signs unfurled,
    No harm now can do;
    He's judged, with all his crew:
  One little word can fell him.

No thanks to them who do their worst,
  The Word can ne'er go under;
Christ comes against their spite accurst,
  With gift and sign and wonder.
    Strip they may of life,
    Goods, name, child, and wife;
    Let them plot and strain!
    They can achieve no gain;
  God's kingdom must stand for us.

TENTH VERSION.

By Frances Eliz. Cox, in " Hymns from the German," London, 1864.

A FORTRESS firm and steadfast Rock
  Is God in time of danger;
A Shield and Sword in every shock
  From foe well known or stranger.

The old foe of man,
Intent on his plan,
With might and with craft
Still plies each deadly shaft;
His like earth saw not ever.

In our own might, so lost our plight,
Our arm no conquest gaineth;
That righteous Man must win the fight
Whom God himself ordaineth.
Thou askest his name?
None else bears the same,—
Christ Jesus the Lord,
As God of hosts adored,
'Tis He must win the battle.

And were the world a hungry crew
Of devils all around us,
Their leaguered host we could subdue,
The thought need not confound us.
The world's vanquished prince
His doom had long since;
His fiercest array
One word of faith can fray,
In spite of threatening gesture.

Unharmed the Word shall yet remain;
For this no thanks they merit;
He aids us on our battle-plain
  With His good gifts and Spirit.
    Then take they our life,
    Wealth, fame, child, and wife;
    No triumph they gain,
    For all their boast is vain,
While ours is still the kingdom.

ELEVENTH VERSION.

From "The Church Book," Philadelphia, 1872.

A MIGHTY Fortress is our God,
  A trusty shield and weapon;
He helps us free from every need
  That hath us now o'ertaken.
    The old bitter foe
    Means us deadly woe:
    Deep guile and great might
    Are his dread arms in fight;
On earth is not his equal.

With might of ours can naught be done,
  Soon were our loss effected;
But for us fights the Valiant One
  Whom God himself elected.
    Ask ye, who is this?
    Jesus Christ it is,
    Of Sabaoth Lord,
    And there's none other God,
  He holds the field forever.

Though devils all the world should fill,
  All watching to devour us,
We tremble not, we fear no ill,
  They cannot overpower us.
    This world's prince may still
    Scowl fierce as he will,
    He can harm us none,
    He's judged, the deed is done,
  One little word o'erthrows him.

The Word they still shall let remain,
  And not a thank have for it;
He's by our side upon the plain,
  With His good gifts and Spirit.

Take they then our life,
Goods, fame, child, and wife;
When their worst is done,
They yet have nothing won,
The kingdom ours remaineth.

TWELFTH VERSION.

From B. H. Kennedy's "Hymnologia Christiana," London, 1863.

A TOWER of strength our God doth stand,
  A buckler to defend us;
In all the woes of life His hand
  True help is nigh to lend us.
Our foe prepares him for the fight,
With cunning armed and hellish might;
  On earth is not his fellow.

With force of arms we nothing can,
  Full soon were we o'erridden;
But for us fights the goodly Man
  Whom God himself hath bidden.
Ask ye his name? 'Tis Christ our Lord,
The God of hosts alone adored,
  Our Champion; none may brave Him.

Should hell's battalions round us press,
   All banded to devour us,
Yet this should work us good success,
   Nor fear e'en then o'erpower us:
Though this world's prince look fierce and bold,
It matters not, his doom is told,
   A single breath can foil him.

Our foes must let the Word stand sure;
   No thanks for this are owing:
God's Spirit makes our way secure,
   His light and strength bestowing.
Those foes may ravish earthly bliss;
Let be, no gain they reap from this:
   God's kingdom still is left us.

THIRTEENTH VERSION.

By Miss Catharine Winkworth, in "Lyra Germanica," I, New York, 1864.

GOD is our stronghold firm and sure,
   Our trusty shield and weapon;
He shall deliver us, whate'er
   Of ill to us may happen.

Our ancient enemy
In earnest now is he;
Much craft and great might
Arm him for the fight;
On earth is not his fellow.

Our might is nought but weakness; soon
 Should we the battle lose,
But for us fights the rightful Man,
 Whom God himself doth choose.
  Askest thou his name?
  'Tis Jesus Christ, the same
  Whom Lord of hosts we call,
  God only over all;
 None from the field can drive Him.

What though the world were full of fiends,
 That would us sheer devour!
We know we yet shall win the day,
 We fear not all their power.
  The prince of this world still
  May struggle as he will;
  He nothing can prevail,
  A word shall make him quail,
 For he is judged of Heaven.

The word of God they shall not touch,
  Yet have no thanks therefor;
God by His Spirit and His gifts
  Is with us in the war.
    Then let them take our life,
    Goods, honor, children, wife;
    Though nought of these we save,
    Small profit shall they have,—
  The kingdom ours abideth.

FOURTEENTH VERSION.

By Miss C. Winkworth, in "Christian Singers of Germany," London, 1869.

A SURE stronghold our God is He,
  A trusty shield and weapon;
Our help He'll be, and set us free,
  Whatever ill may happen.
    That old malicious foe
    Intends us deadly woe;
    Armed with the strength of hell,
    And deepest craft as well,
  On earth is not his fellow.

Through our own force we nothing can,
    Straight were we lost forever;
But for us fights the proper Man,
    By God sent to deliver.
        Ask ye who this may be?
        Christ Jesus named is He,
        Of Sabaoth the Lord,
        Sole God to be adored;
    'Tis He must win the battle.

And were the world with devils filled,
    All eager to devour us,
Our souls to fear should little yield,
    They cannot overpower us.
        Their dreaded prince no more
        Can harm us as of yore;
        Look grim as e'er he may,
        Doomed is his ancient sway;
    A word can overthrow him.

Still shall they leave that Word its might,
    And yet no thanks shall merit;
Still is He with us in the fight
    By His good gifts and Spirit.

E'en should they take our life,
Goods, honor, children, wife,
Though all of these were gone,
Yet nothing have they won,—
God's kingdom ours abideth.

FIFTEENTH VERSION.

By R. Massie, "Spiritual Songs of Luther," London, 1854.

A CASTLE is our God, a tower,
A shield and trusty weapon;
He saveth us by His strong power
From all the ills that happen.
The old arch-fiend, I trow,
Is in good earnest now;
Great might and cunning are
His panoply of war;
On earth there is none like him.

Stood we alone in our own might,
Full sure were we of losing;
For us the one true Man doth fight,
The Man of God's own choosing.

Dost thou inquire his name?
Christ Jesus we proclaim,
The God who armies guides,
There is no God besides;
In every field He triumphs.

What tho' the world should swarm with fiends
  Eager to tear and rend us?
We will not fear, if God befriends,
  Success shall yet attend us.
    The prince who rules below
    No harm can do us, though
    He looks so fierce and grim,
    For Christ hath judgèd him;
A little word can slay him.

Leave us they must Thy blessed Word,
  For which no thanks they merit;
With us abideth still the Lord,
  His gifts and Holy Spirit.
    Take, if they will, our life,
    Goods, honor, child, and wife;
    We freely let them go;
    They profit not the foe;
With us remains the kingdom.

SIXTEENTH VERSION.

J. C. Jacobi, "Psalmodia Germanica," I, p. 83.

God is our Refuge in distress,
    Our strong defence and armor;
He 's present, when left comfortless,
    In raging storms our harbor.
        Th' infernal enemy,
        Look! how enraged is he!
        He now exerts his force
        To stop the Gospel-course;
    Who can withstand this tyrant?

All human power must here be lost;
    Our strength would soon be moved;
The *Valiant Man*, of whom we boast,
    Is Christ the well-beloved:
        This is the Conqueror
        Endowed with foreign power,
        The Lord both great and good,
        And only living God,
    He gains the field of battle.

THE TRIUMPH OF FAITH.

If all the devils should wage the fight
  In order to destroy us,
They would not put us into fright,
  The victory should be joyous.
    We scorn the prince of hell;
    With fury let him swell;
    He cannot hurt one hair,
    We shall escape his snare,
  One single word can rout him.

This word puts all our foes to flight,
  With shame they are confounded,
For Christ instructs our hands to fight,
  His Spirit is unbounded.
    Tho' we should lose our lives,
    Fame, children, goods, and wives,
    Destroying all they can,
    They'll find but little gain—
  God's kingdom is our portion.

The Church.

Es spricht der Unweisen Mund.

PARAPHRASE OF THE FOURTEENTH PSALM.

By R. Massie, "Spiritual Songs."

THE mouth of fools doth God confess,
  But while their lips draw nigh Him
Their heart is full of wickedness,
  And all their deeds deny Him.
Corrupt are they, and every one
Abominable deeds hath done;
  There is not one well-doer.

The Lord looked down from His high tower
  On all mankind below him,
To see if any owned His power,
  And truly sought to know Him;
Who all their understanding bent
To search His holy Word, intent
  To do His will in earnest.

But none there was who walked with God,
  For all aside had slidden,
Delusive paths of folly trod,
  And followed lusts forbidden;
Not one there was who practiced good,
And yet they deemed, in haughty mood,
  Their deeds must surely please Him.

How long, by folly blindly led,
  Will ye oppress the needy,
And eat my people up like bread?
  So fierce are ye and greedy!
In God they put no trust at all,
Nor will on Him in trouble call,
  But be their own providers.

Therefore their heart is never still,
  A falling leaf dismays them;
God is with him who doth His will,
  Who trusts Him and obeys Him;
But ye the poor man's hope despise,
And laugh at him, e'en when he cries,
  That God is his sure comfort.

Who shall to Israel's outcast race
  From Zion bring salvation?

God will himself at length show grace,
   And loose the captive nation;
That will He do by Christ their King;
   Let Jacob then be glad and sing,
      And Israel be joyful.

(J. C. Jacobi, "Psalmodia Germanica," II, p. 66.)

THE foolish men profanely boast
   Of God and true religion;
Their faithless heart is full of lust,
   Their life's a contradiction:
Corrupted is their very fame,
God's holiness abhors the same,
   There's none doth good, but evil.

The Lord from his celestial throne
   Looked down on every creature,
To find one man who had begun
   To love God's holy nature;
But all the race was gone astray,
All had forsook the saving way
   Of God his Revelation.

How long will they be ignorant
    Of their abomination?
Who thus despise my covenant,
    Nor spare my holy nation?
They never call upon the Lord,
Put all their trust upon their hoard,
    And turn their own defenders.

Yet is their heart in constant pain,
    And secret fear and trembling;
God with His Zion will remain,
    Where saints are still assembling:
But you deride the poor's advice,
His greatest comfort you despise,
    That God's his only refuge.

O that the joyful day would come
    To turn our desolation,
When God will bring His children home,
    And finish our salvation!
Then shall the tribes of Jacob sing,
And Judah praise their Lord and King,
    With lasting hallelujahs.

Psalm 12. *Salvum me fac.*

Ach Gott vom Himmel sieh darein.

(Cox, "Sacred Hymns from the German.")

Look down, O Lord, from heaven behold,
   And let Thy pity waken!
How few the flock within Thy fold,
   Neglected and forsaken!
Almost thou'lt seek for faith in vain,
And those who should Thy truth maintain
   Thy Word from us have taken.

With frauds which they themselves invent
   Thy truth they have confounded;
Their hearts are not with one consent
   On thy pure doctrine grounded;
And, whilst they gleam with outward show,
They lead Thy people to and fro,
   In error's maze astounded.

God surely will uproot all those
   With vain deceits who store us,
With haughty tongue who God oppose,
   And say, "Who'll stand before us?

By right or might we will prevail;
What we determine cannot fail,
   For who can lord it o'er us?"

For this, saith God, I will arise,
   These wolves my flock are rending;
I've heard my people's bitter sighs
   To heaven my throne ascending:
Now will I up, and set at rest
Each weary soul by fraud opprest,
   The poor with might defending.

The silver seven times tried is pure
   From all adulteration;
So, through God's word, shall men endure
   Each trial and temptation:
Its worth gleams brighter through the cross,
And, purified from human dross,
   It shines through every nation.

Thy truth Thou wilt preserve, O Lord,
   Pure from their artful glozing;
Oh! make us lean upon Thy word,
   With hearts unmoved reposing,
Though bad men triumph, and their crew
Are gathered round, the faithful few
   With crafty toils inclosing.

(J. C. Jacobi, "Psalmodia Germanica," I, p. 93.)

O LORD, in mercy cast an eye
  On Thy distressèd Zion;
How few of Christians can'st thou spy
  That 'scape th' infernal lion?
Thy truth was never more despised
Faith, charity is but disguised
  Amongst its mere professors.

They teach but lies and flattery,
  What is their own invention;
Their doctrine is but mockery
  Of God and His intention:
One chooses this, another that,
Pretending to they know not what,
  Though saint-like in appearance.

Root out all mere formality,
  O Lord! and its infection;
Confound refined hypocrisy,
  Which is beyond correction:
Yet shall our words be free, they cry;
Where is the Lord will ask us why?
  Who dare control our sayings?

The Lord, who sees the poor opprest,
    And hears these proud professors,
Will rise to give His children rest,
    And curb their sore oppressors;
Nor will He send His word in vain,
But wilful mockers shall be slain,
    To save His poor beloved.

As silver seven times purified
    Shines in its greatest beauty,
So, Lord, thy Word, though often tried,
    Shall still exert its duty:
Affliction shall refine it more,
And show its energy and power,
    According to Thy promise.

O Lord! we pray, preserve it pure
    In this our generation,
And let us dwell in Thee, secure
    From all abomination:
For sin increases every day,
Where vile blasphemers bear the sway
    In church or state soever.

PSALM 124. *Nisi quia Dominus.*
Wär' Gott nicht mit uns diese Zeit.
(R. Massie, "Spiritual Songs," p. 35.)

HAD God not come, may Israel say,
    Had God not come to aid us,
Our enemies on that sad day
    Would surely have dismayed us;
A remnant now, and handful small,
Held in contempt and scorn by all
    Who cruelly oppress us.

Their furious wrath, did God permit,
    Would quickly have consumed us,
And in the deep and yawning pit
    With life and limb entombed us;
Like men o'er whom dark waters roll,
The streams had gone e'en o'er our soul,
    And mightily o'erwhelmed us.

Thanks be to God, who from the pit
    Snatched us, when it was gaping;
Our souls, like birds that break the net,
    To the blue skies escaping;
The snare is broken—we are free!
The Lord our helper praised be,
    The God of earth and heaven.

Grace.

Nun freut euch, lieben Christen g'mein.

A THANKSGIVING FOR THE HIGHEST BENEFITS WHICH GOD HAS SHOWN US IN CHRIST.

An eye-witness of the Reformation says of that hymn: "Who can doubt that by this hymn many hundreds of Christians have been converted to the faith of Jesus, who had never before heard of the name of Luther? But his noble and dear words won their hearts over to the reception of the truth; so that, in my opinion, the spiritual songs have contributed not a little to the spread of the Gospel." To this we may add: "Luther," said the Romanists, "has done us more harm by his songs than by his sermons."

(C. Winkworth, "Christian Singers of Germany.")

DEAR Christian people, now rejoice!
Our hearts within us leap,

While we, as with one soul and voice,
    With love and gladness deep,
Tell how our God beheld our need,
And sing that sweet and wondrous deed,
    That hath so dearly cost Him.

Captive to Satan once I lay,
    In inner death forlorn;
My sins oppressed me night and day,
    Therein I had been born,
And deeper fell howe'er I strove;
My life had neither joy nor love,
    So sore had sin possessed me.

My good works could avail me naught,
    For they with sin were stained;
My will against God's justice fought,
    And dead to good remained;
My anguish drove me to despair,
For death I knew was waiting there,
    And what but hell was left me?

Then God in His eternity
    Looked on my boundless woe,
His deep compassions flowed toward me,
    True succor to bestow:

His Father's heart did yearn and melt
To heal the bitter pains I felt,
   Though it should cost His dearest.

He spake to His beloved Son:
" Go Thou, my heart's bright crown,
The time for pity is begun,
   Go Thou in mercy down
To break for men Sin's heavy chain,
To end for them Death's hopeless reign,
   And give them life eternal."

The Son delighteth to obey,
   And born of virgin mother,
Awhile on this low earth did stay,
   And thus became my brother:
His mighty power He hidden bore,
A servant's form like mine He wore,
   My foe for me to vanquish.

To me He spake: " Hold fast by Me,
   And thou shalt conquer now;
Myself I wholly give for thee,
   For thee I wrestle now;
For I am with thee, thou art Mine,
Henceforth My place is also thine,
   The foe shall never part us.

"I know that he will shed My blood,
　And take My life away;
But I will bear it for thy good,
　Only believe away:
Death swallows up this life of Mine,
My innocence—all sins of thine,
　And so art thou delivered.

"And when I rise to heaven above,
　Where is my Father's home,
I still will be thy Lord in love,
　And bid my Spirit come
To solace thee in every woe,
To teach thee Me aright to know,
　And into truth to guide thee.

"And even as I have done and said,
　So shalt thou say and do,
That so God's kingdom may be spread,
　And He have honor due:
And this last counsel give I thee,
From men's additions keep thou free
　The treasure I have left thee."

(J. C. Jacobi, "Psalmodia Germanica," I, p. 30.)

Now come, ye Christians all, and bring,
    With cheerful hearts and voices,
Due praises to our God and King,
    Whose holy court rejoices
To see the wonders of this love,
Which brought Redemption from above,
    Beyond our expectation.

As Satan's slave in sin I lay,
    Despairing of salvation,
Original sin had got the sway,
    God was my detestation;
And sinking deeper by degrees
Into this desperate disease,
    I must be lost forever.

Good works would here not serve my turn,
    They could produce no merit;
Rebellion made my free-will burn
    Against the Holy Spirit.
My anguish drove me to despair,
Death was my mirror everywhere,
    The presage of hell-torment.

But, O unutterable grace,
    That pitied my condition,
Th' eternal Son would take my place,
    To save me from perdition;
Down to this world the Saviour flies,
Stretches His willing arms, and dies
    For me a wretched sinner.

Justice was pleased to bruise the God,
    And author of salvation,
To pay its wrongs with heavenly blood,
    And quench hell and damnation;
Infinite racks and pangs He bore,
And rose; the law could ask no more
    Of this my Mediator.

Thus the Redeemer spake to me,
    In smiling condescension:
"I wholly give Myself for thee
    To unveil this My intention,
That I am thine with all I have,
And purchased by the cross and grave,
    No foe shall disunite us.

"I'll rise again, retake the crown
    And glory of my Father,

From thence I'll send my Spirit down
    To bring my saints together;
His comforts shall abide with thee,
To strengthen thy belief in Me,
    And seal thy sure salvation.

" What I have suffered, done, and taught,
    Shall be thy rule of action,
That all thy neighbors may be brought
    To follow My direction.
Beware of other guides of faith,
Stick to My self-denying path,
    The safest way to glory."

PSALM 128. *Beati omnes qui timent Deum.*

Wohl dem, der in Gottesfurcht steht.

(R. Massie, "Spiritual Songs," p. 51.)

HAPPY the man who feareth God,
Whose feet His holy ways have trod;
Thine own good hand shall nourish thee,
And well and happy shalt thou be.

Thy wife shall, like a fruitful vine,
Fill all thy house with clusters fine ;
Thy children all be fresh and sound,
Like olive-plants thy table round.

Lo! to the man these blessings cleave
Who in God's holy fear doth live ;
From him the ancient curse hath fled
By Adam's race inherited.

Out of Mount Zion God shall send,
And crown with joy thy latter end ;
That thou Jerusalem mayst see
In favor and prosperity.

He shall be with thee in thy ways,
And give thee health and length of days ;
Yea, thou shalt children's children see,
And peace on Israel shall be.
      Amen.

Ps. 67. *Deus misereatur nostri.*

Es wolt uns Gott genædig sein.

(Mills, " Horæ Germanicæ," p. 201.)

To us, O God, impart Thy grace,
    Thy Holy Spirit sending;
So cheer us with Thy smiling face,
    A pledge of life unending,
That we may learn what Thou hast wrought,
    What best will meet Thy pleasure;
Then, of the bliss by Jesus bought,
    To heathens teach the measure,
That they, too, may enjoy it.

The heathen, from their idols free,
    Their thanks and honors bringing,
And all the world, shall yet in Thee
    Rejoice, with rapture singing—
" Thou art our Ruler here below,
    And sin no more shall lead us;
Thy word the path of peace will show,
    With bread of life will feed us,—
And bring our souls to heaven."

O when will all the nations learn
  To praise Thee by well-doing!
The earth to Thee from error turn,
  Her tribes Thy grace pursuing!
Now bless us, Father and the Son,
  And bless us, Holy Spirit!
By all to Thee be honors done,
  As well Thy favors merit!
Amen, Lord! Hallelujah!

Law.

Mensch willt du leben seliglich.
(R. Massie, "Spiritual Songs," p. 53.)

THIS is the shorter paraphrase of the Decalogue.

WILT thou, O man, live happily,
And dwell with God eternally,
The ten commandments keep, for thus
Our God himself commanded us.
   Kyrie eleison.

I am the Lord and God! take heed
No other god doth thee mislead;
Thy heart shall trust alone in me,
Yea, mine own kingdom thou shalt be.
   Kyrie eleison.

Honor my Name in word and deed,
And call on Me in time of need:
Keep holy, too, the Sabbath day,
That work in thee I also may.
   Kyrie eleison.

Obedient always, next to Me,
To father and to mother be:
Kill no man; even anger dread:
Keep undefiled thy marriage bed.
      Kyrie eleison.

Steal not, nor do thy neighbor wrong
By bearing witness with false tongue:
Thy neighbor's wife desire thou not,
Nor grudge him aught that he hath got.
      Kyrie eleison.

Diess sind die heiligen zehn Gebot.

(R. Massie, "Spiritual Songs," p. 57.)

THIS is the larger form of the ten commandments.

THAT men a godly life might live,
God did these ten commandments give
By His true servant Moses, high
Upon the mount of Sinai.
      Kyrie eleison.

I am thy God and Lord alone,
No other God besides Me own;
Put thy whole confidence in Me,
And love Me in sincerity.
    Kyrie eleison.

By idle word and speech profane
Take not My holy name in vain;
And praise not aught as good and true
But what God doth both say and do.
    Kyrie eleison.

Hallow the day which God hath blest,
That thou and all thy house may rest;
Keep hand and heart from labor free,
That God may have His work in thee.
    Kyrie eleison.

Give to thy parents honor due,
Be dutiful, and loving too;
And help them when their strength decays;
So shall God give thee length of days.
    Kyrie eleison.

Harbor no hatred, nor ill will,
Lest hate breed anger, and thou kill;
Be patient and of gentle mood,
And to thine enemy do good.
    Kyrie eleison.

Be faithful to thy marriage vows,
Thy heart give only to thy spouse;
Keep thy life pure, and lest thou sin
Use temperance and discipline.
    Kyrie eleison.

Steal not; oppressive acts abhor;
Nor wring their life-blood from the poor;
But open wide thy loving hand
To all the needy in the land.
    Kyrie eleison.

Bear not false witness, nor belie
Thy neighbor by foul calumny;
Defend his innocence from blame,
And hide with charity his shame.
    Kyrie eleison.

Thy neighbor's wife desire thou not,
His house, nor aught that he hath got;
But wish that his such good may be
As thine own heart doth wish for thee.
    Kyrie eleison.

God these commandments gave, therein
To show thee, son of man, thy sin,
And make thee also well perceive
How unto God man ought to live.
    Kyrie eleison.

Help us, Lord Jesus Christ, for we
A Mediator have in Thee;
Without Thy help our works are vain,
And merit only endless pain.
    Kyrie eleison.

The Creed.

Wir glauben all an einen Gott.

("Choral Book," Appendix VI.)

WE all believe in One true God,
    Maker of the earth and heaven;
The Father, who to us in love
    Hath the claim of children given.
He in soul and body feeds us,
    All we want His hand provides us;
Thro' all snares and perils leads us,
    Watches that no harm betides us;
He cares for us, cares for us by day and night,
All things are governed by His might.

And we believe in Jesus Christ,
    His only Son, our Lord, possessing
An equal Godhead, throne and might,
    Thro' whom descends the Father's blessing;

Conceivèd of the Holy Spirit,
   Born of Mary, virgin mother;
That lost man might life inherit
   Made true man, our elder Brother,
Was crucified for sinful men,
And raised by God to life again.

And we confess the Holy Ghost,
   Who from Son and Father floweth, ·
The Comforter of fearful hearts,
   Who all precious gifts bestoweth;
In whom all the Church hath union,
Who maintains the saints' communion;
We believe our sins forgiven,
And that life with God in heaven,
When we are raised again, shall be
Our portion in eternity.

The Lord's Prayer.

Vater unser im Himmelreich.

A PIOUS man in Venice, upon reading Luther's Paraphrase of the Lord's Prayer, without knowing its author, is said to have cried out, " Blessed is the womb that bare thee, and the paps which thou hast sucked!"

<small>(C. Winkworth, "Choral Book for England," No. 114.)</small>

OUR Father, thou in heaven above,
Who biddest us to dwell in love,
As brethren of one family,
And cry for all we need to Thee;
Teach us to mean the words we say,
And from the inmost heart to pray.

All hallowed be Thy name, O Lord!
Oh, let us firmly keep Thy Word,

And lead, according to Thy name,
A holy life, untouched by blame;
Let no false teachings do us hurt,—
All poor deluded souls convert.

Thy kingdom come! Thine let it be
In time, and through eternity!
Oh, let thy Holy Spirit dwell
With us, to rule and guide us well;
From Satan's mighty power and rage
Preserve Thy Church from age to age.

Thy will be done on earth, O Lord,
As where in heaven Thou art adored!
Patience in time of grief bestow,
Obedience true through weal and woe;
Strength, tempting wishes to control
That thwart Thy will within the soul.

Give us to-day our daily bread,
Let us be duly clothed and fed,
And keep Thou from our homes afar
Famine and pestilence and war,
That we may live in godly peace,
Unvexed by cares and avarice,

Forgive us our sins, that they no more
May grieve and haunt us as before,
As we forgive their trespasses
Who unto us have done amiss;
Thus let us dwell in charity,
And serve each other willingly.

Into temptation lead us not;
And when the foe doth war and plot
Against our souls on every hand,
Then, armed with faith, oh may we stand
Against him as a valiant host,
Through comfort of the Holy Ghost.

Deliver us from evil, Lord!
The days are dark and foes abroad;
Redeem us from the second death;
And when we yield our dying breath,
Console us, grant us calm release,
And take our souls to Thee in peace.

Amen! that is, So let it be!
Strengthen our faith and trust in Thee,

That we may doubt not, but believe
That what we ask we shall receive;
Thus in Thy name and at Thy word
We say Amen, now hear us, Lord!

(J. C. Jacobi, " Psalmodia Germanica," I, p. 65.)

Our Father! who from heaven above
Bid'st us to live in constant love
As brethren, and in truth to join
T' adore this Father-Name of thine,
Grant we may always pray to Thee
In spirit and sincerity.

Thy Name be hallowed everywhere;
Make us to read Thy Word with care,
That we may live accordingly,
And praise Thy sacred Name on high;
From all false doctrine, self-conceit,
Thy poor deluded flock retreat.

Thy kingdom come, thy grace be nigh,
O'er all the earth, o'er all the sky;

The Holy Spirit of thy grace
Bestow His gifts on human race;
From Satan's woful tyranny
Keep all Thy churches safe and free.

Thy will be done in earth, as well
As 'tis in heaven, where angels dwell;
In joy and sorrow make our mind
Be cheerfully to Thee resigned:
All motions of our flesh and blood
Subdue, when Thy will is withstood.

Give us this day our daily bread,
And what we want for present need;
From sad contention, war, and strife,
From dearth and pest, remove our life.
Preserve our peace and liberty;
From filthy lucre make us free.

Forgive us all our trespasses,
That are so great and numberless;
And make us willing to forgive
Our enemies with whom we live:
Let mutual love and charity
Unite Thy Christian family.

Into temptation lead us not
When Satan lays his secret plot,
But lend us Thine almighty hand
To fight with courage, and withstand;
That, armed with faith as with a shield,
We may at last obtain the field.

At length begin to set us free
From sin and all its misery;
Redeem us from eternal death,
Thy grace relieve our dying breath:
A blessed exit be our doom,
To bring us t' our eternal home.

For Thine 's the power and majesty,
Now, and to all eternity:
Increase our faith and guide our ways,
And give us grace Thy name to praise:
According to Thy sacred Word,
A blessed *Amen* us afford.

Prayer.

Verleih uns Frieden gnaediglich.

(R. Massie, "Spiritual Songs," p. 68.)

In these our days so perilous,
Lord, peace in mercy send us;
No God but Thou can fight for us,
No God but Thou defend us,
Our only God and Saviour.

Baptism.

A SPIRITUAL SONG CONCERNING OUR HOLY BAPTISM.

Christ unser Herr zum Jordan ging.

(R. Massie, "Spiritual Songs," p. 69.)

To Jordan came our Lord the Christ,
  To do God's pleasure willing,
And there was by Saint John baptized,
  All righteousness fulfilling;
There did He consecrate a bath
  To wash away transgression,
And quench the bitterness of death
  By His own blood and passion;
He would a new life give us.

So hear ye all, and well perceive
  What God doth call Baptism,
And what a Christian should believe
  Who error shuns and schism:

That we should water use, the Lord
 Declareth it His pleasure ;
Not simple water, but the Word
 And Spirit without measure ;
He is the true Baptizer.

To show us this, He hath His Word
 With signs and symbols given ;
On Jordan's banks was plainly heard
 The Father's voice from heaven :
"This is my well-beloved Son,
 In whom my soul delighteth ;
Hear Him." Yea, hear Him every one
 Whom He himself inviteth,
Hear and obey His teaching.

In tender manhood Jesus straight
 To holy Jordan wendeth ;
The Holy Ghost from heaven's gate
 In dovelike shape descendeth ;
That thus the truth be not denied,
 Nor should our faith e'er waver,
That the Three Persons all preside
 At Baptism's holy laver,
And dwell with the believer.

Thus Jesus his disciples sent:
  Go, teach ye every nation,
That lost in sin they must repent,
  And flee from condemnation:
He that believes and is baptized,
  Obtains a mighty blessing;
A new-born man, no more he dies,
  Eternal life possessing,
A joyful heir of heaven.

Who in this mercy hath not faith,
  Nor aught therein discerneth,
Is yet in sin, condemned to death,
  And fire that ever burneth;
His holiness avails him not,
  Nor aught which he is doing;
His birth-sin brings it all to naught,
  And maketh sure his ruin;
Himself he cannot succor.

The eye of sense alone is dim,
  And nothing sees but water;
Faith sees Christ Jesus, and in Him
  The lamb ordained for slaughter;

She sees the cleansing fountain red
With the dear blood of Jesus,
Which from the sins inherited
From fallen Adam frees us,
And those we have committed.

Repentance.

A PARAPHRASE OF THE 130TH PSALM.

Aus tiefer Noth schrei ich zu dir.

FIRST VERSION.

By C. Winkworth, "Lyra Germanica," First Series, p. 65.

OUT of the depth I cry to Thee,
   Lord God, oh hear my prayer!
Incline a gracious ear to me,
   And bid me not despair:
If Thou rememberest each misdeed,
If each should have its rightful meed,
   Lord, who shall stand before Thee?

Lord, through Thy love alone we gain
   The pardon of our sin;
The strictest life is but in vain,
   Our works can nothing win;

That none should boast himself of aught,
But own in fear Thy grace hath wrought
What in him seemeth righteous.

Wherefore my hope is in the Lord,
  My works I count but dust;
I build not there, but on His Word,
  And in His goodness trust.
Up to His care myself I yield,
He is my tower, my rock, my shield,
  And for His help I tarry.

And though it tarry till the night,
  And round again to morn,
My heart shall ne'er mistrust Thy might,
  Nor count itself forlorn.
Do thus, O ye of Israel's seed,
Ye of the Spirit born indeed,
  Wait for your God's appearing.

Though great our sins and sore our wounds,
  And deep and dark our fall,
His helping mercy hath no bounds,
  His love surpasseth all.

Our trusty, loving Shepherd he,
Who shall at last set Israel free
From all their sin and sorrow.

SECOND VERSION.

(J. C. Jacobi, "Psalmodia Germanica," I, p. 61.)

Out of the deeps of long distress,
  The borders of despairing,
I send my cries to seek Thy grace,
  My groans to move Thy hearing;
Great God! should Thy severer eye
Mark and revenge iniquity,
  Who could abide Thy judgment?

But Thou hast built the throne of grace
  Free to dispense Thy favor,
That sinners may approach Thy face
  To ease their mournful labor;
For pardon is with Thee our God,
Thy Son has sealed it with His blood;
  This is our only refuge.

In Thee alone I put my trust,
    And only plead Thy merit,
For Thou art kind as well as just,—
    Thee I adore in spirit;
Nor shall I trust Thy Word in vain,
'Tis the relief from all my pain,
    When living or when dying.

Just as the guards that keep the night
    Long for the rising morning,
So wait I for Thy gracious light,
    Of which Thou gav'st me warning:
Then let the sons of *Israel* wait
On God before His holy gate
    Till He display His blessing.

There 's full redemption at His throne,
    For loads of black transgression;
He pardons what our hands have done
    When Christ makes intercession:
Great is His love and large his grace;
He turns our feet from sinful ways,
    And *Israel* shall be saved.

THIRD VERSION.

(Mills, "Horæ Germanicæ," p. 71.)

From deep distress to Thee I pray,
   O God, hear my entreaty!
Turn not Thy face from me away,
   But show Thy tender pity:
As Judge, should Thou my deeds regard,
In justice weighing due award,
   How could I stand the trial?

With Thee should mercy not prevail
   To show to man Thy favor,
His every act his guilt would swell,—
   Vain were his best endeavor.
His goodness in its utmost length
Reveals his utter want of strength,—
   He must rely on mercy.

On God alone, and on His grace,
   Can I securely rest me;
He sees my heart, He heals distress,—
   To Him, then, why not trust me?
He owns a Father's name, and knows
The full amount of human woes;
   On Him be my reliance!

Should comfort seem afar to keep,
   I'll not sink down despairing;
They who in godly sorrow weep
   Shall find a gracious hearing:
Thus Christians do, and they are blest
In God, their confidence and rest,
   Their comfort and Redeemer.

Many and great the sins I own,
   But greater God's free mercies:
From wrath I flee to His dear Son,
   Who bore for me its curses:
And He will be my Shepherd, too,
With all my troubles guide me through,
   To rest with Him in glory.

FOURTH VERSION.

(Moravian Hymn-Book, No. 240, abr.)

OUT of the deep I cry to Thee,
   My God, with heart's contrition;
Bow down Thine ear in grace to me,
   And hear Thou my petition:

For if in judgment Thou wilt try
Man's sin and great iniquity,
  Ah, who can stand before Thee?

To gain remission of our sin
  No work of ours availeth;
God's favor we may strive to win,
  But all our labor faileth;
We're 'midst our fairest actions lost,
And none 'fore Him of aught can boast:
  We live alone through mercy.

Therefore my hope is in His grace,
  And not in my own merit;
On Him my confidence I place,
  Instructed by His Spirit:
His precious Word hath promised me
He will my joy and comfort be;
  Thereon is my reliance.

Though sin with us doth much abound,
  Yet grace still more aboundeth;
Sufficient help in Christ is found
  Where sin most deeply woundeth:
He the good Shepherd is indeed,
Who His lost sheep doth seek and lead
  With tender love and pity.

The Lord's Supper.

Jesus Christus, unser Heiland der von uns.

(R. Massie, "Spiritual Songs," p. 75.)

CHRIST, who freed our souls from danger,
And hath turned away God's anger,
Suffered pains no tongue can tell,
To redeem us from pains of hell.

That we never might forget it,
Take my flesh, He said, and eat it,
Hidden in this piece of bread,
Drink my blood in this wine, He said.

Whoso to this board repaireth,
Take good heed how he prepareth;
Death instead of life shall he
Find, who cometh unworthily.

Praise the Father, God in heaven,
Who such dainty food hath given,
And for misdeeds thou hast done
Gave to die His beloved Son.

Trust God's Word; it is intended
For the sick who would be mended;
Those whose heavy-laden breast
Groans with sin, and is seeking rest.

To such grace and mercy turneth
Every soul that truly mourneth;
Art thou well? Avoid this board,
Else thou reapest an ill reward.

Lo! He saith himself, " Ye weary,
Come to me and I will cheer ye;"
Needless were the leech's skill
To the souls that be strong and well.

Couldst thou earn thine own salvation,
Useless were my death and passion;
Wilt thou thine own helper be?
No meet table is this for thee.

If thou this believest truly,
And confession makest duly,
Thou a welcome guest art here,
This rich banquet thy soul shall cheer.

Sweet henceforth shall be thy labor,
Thou shalt truly love thy neighbor,
So shall he both taste and see
What thy Saviour hath done in thee.

Gott sei gelobet und gebenedeiet.

(R. Massie, "Spiritual Songs," p. 78.)

Strophe.

MAY God be praised henceforth and blest forever!
Who, Himself both gift and giver,
With His own flesh and blood our souls doth nourish;
May they grow thereby and flourish!
Kyrie eleison.

Antistrophe.

By Thy holy body, Lord, the same
Which from Thine own mother Mary came;
By the drops which Thou didst bleed,
Help us in the hour of need!
    Kyrie eleison.

Strophe.

Thou hast to death Thy holy body given,
Life to win for us in heaven;
By stronger love, dear Lord, Thou couldst
  not bind us,
Whereof this should well remind us.
    Kyrie eleison.

Antistrophe.

Lord, Thy love constrained Thee for our good
Mighty things to do by Thy dear blood;
Thou hast paid the debt we owed,
Thou hast made our peace with God.
    Kyrie eleison.

Strophe.

May God bestow on us His grace and blessing,
That, His holy footsteps tracing,

We walk as brethren dear in love and union,
Nor repent this sweet communion.
    Kyrie eleison.

Antistrophe.

Let not us the Holy Ghost forsake ;
May He grant that we the right way take ;
That poor Christendom may see
Days of peace and unity.
    Kyrie eleison.

Death.

Mitten wir im Leben sind.

THIS hymn is one of those founded on a more ancient hymn of Notker, a learned Benedictine of St. Gall, who died in 912. The original has only one verse, and runs thus:

> "Media vita in morte sumus.
> Quem quærimus adjutorem
> Nisi te, domine?
> Qui pro peccatis nostris
> Juste irasceris.
> Sancte deus, sancte fortis,
> Sancte et misericors salvator:
> Amaræ morti ne tradas nos."

Luther, however, enlarged it, in the form as it is found in German hymn-books. Notker is said to have composed it while watching some workmen who were building the bridge of Martinsbruck at the peril of their lives. It was soon set to music, and became universally known; indeed, it was used as a battle-song, until the custom was forbidden on account of its being supposed to exercise magical influences. In a German version it formed part of the service for the burial of the dead as early as the thirteenth century, and is still preserved, in an unmetrical form, in the burial service of the Episcopal Church.

(Winkworth, "Lyra Germanica," I, p. 235.)

> In the midst of life, behold
>   Death has girt us round;
> Whom for help then shall we pray,
>   Where shall grace be found?
> In Thee, O Lord, alone!
> We rue the evil we have done,
> That Thy wrath on us hath drawn.
>   Holy Lord and God!
>   Strong and holy God!
>   Merciful and holy Saviour!
>   Eternal God!
> Sink us not beneath
> Bitter pains of endless death.
>   Kyrie eleison!
>
> In the midst of death the jaws
>   Of hell against us gape;
> Who from peril dire as this
>   Openeth us escape?

'Tis Thou, O Lord, alone!
Our bitter suffering and our sin
Pity from Thy mercy win.
  Holy Lord and God!
  Strong and holy God!
  Merciful and holy Saviour!
  Eternal God!
Let us not despair
For the fire that burneth there.
     Kyrie eleison!

In the midst of hell our sins
 Drive us to despair;
Whither shall we flee from them?
 Where is refuge, where?
In Thee, Lord Christ, alone!
For Thou hast shed Thy precious blood,
All our sins Thou makest good.
  Holy Lord and God!
  Strong and holy God!
  Merciful and holy Saviour!
  Eternal God!
Let us never fall
From the true faith's hope for all.
     Kyrie eleison!

Mit Fried und Freud fahr ich dahin.

(C. Winkworth, "Christian Singers of Germany," p. 114.)

In peace and joy I now depart,
   According to God's will;
For full of comfort is my heart,
   So calm and still.
So doth God his promise keep,
And death to me is but a sleep.

'Tis Christ has wrought this work for me;
   Thy dear and only Son,
Whom Thou hast suffered me to see,
   And made Him known
As our Help when woes are rife,
And e'en in death itself our Life.

For Thou in mercy unto all
   Hast set this Saviour forth,
And to His kingdom Thou dost call
   The whole sad earth,
Through Thy blessed, wholesome Word,
That now in every place is heard.

He is the Hope, the saving Light,
　That heathen nations need;
And those who know Thee not aright
　Will teach and lead;
While His Israel's joy He is,
His people's glory, praise, and bliss.

Praise.

Jesaja, dem Propheten, das geschah.

ISAIAH 6 : 1-4.

(R. Massie, "Spiritual Songs," p. 85.)

THESE things the seer Isaiah did befall:
In spirit he beheld the Lord of all
On a high throne, raised up in splendor bright,
His garment's border filled the choir with light.
Beside Him stood two seraphim, which had
Six wings, wherewith they both alike were clad:
With twain they hid their shining face, with twain
They hid their feet as with a flowing train,
And with the other twain they both did fly.
One to the other thus aloud did cry,—
"Holy is God, the Lord of Sabaoth!
Holy is God, the Lord of Sabaoth!
Holy is God, the Lord of Sabaoth!
His glory filleth all the trembling earth."
With the loud cry the posts and thresholds shook,
And the whole house was filled with mist and smoke.

The Te Deum.

Herr Gott, dich loben wir.

THIS hymn Luther translated from the Latin of St. Ambrose. Mr. Saunders, in his *Evenings with the Sacred Poets*, p. 33, says, "that according to tradition, this grand anthem gushed forth in sudden inspiration from the lips of Ambrose as he baptized Augustine; or other authorities, who reject the legend, believe it to have sprung from an earlier Oriental hymn. If so, might it not possibly have formed part of the worship of the primitive Christians, who, in the time of Pliny, 'met before dawn, to sing hymns to Christ as God?' (Carmenque Christo, quasi Deo! lib. x.) That same 'Te Deum' has accompanied many a martyr to the stake in Flanders, Bavaria, Germany, England, and elsewhere. It was the English Bishop Fisher's farewell as he stood beside the block. Once it was lifted up where no lesser hymn would have been fitting,— when Columbus discovered the first gray outline of the New World, and 'the crew threw themselves into each others' arms, weeping for joy!' There is an old custom still perpetuated at Magdalen College, Oxford, at the dawn of May Day, when the 'Te Deum' is sung in the original Latin, from the tower of the college."

(Moravian Hymn-Book, No. 554.)

LORD GOD, thy praise we sing,
To Thee our thanks we bring;
Both heaven and earth do worship Thee,
Thou Father of eternity:
To Thee all angels loudly cry,
The heavens and all the powers on high:
Cherubs and seraphs Thee proclaim,
And cry thrice holy to Thy name:
    Holy is our Lord God,
    Holy is our Lord God,
    Holy is our Lord God,
    The Lord of Sabaoth!

With splendor of Thy glory spread
Are heaven and earth replenished;
The apostles' glorious company,
The prophets' fellowship praise Thee;

The noble and victorious host
Of martyrs make of Thee their boast;
The holy Church in every place
Throughout the earth exalts Thy praise.
Thee, Father, God on heaven's throne,
Thy only and beloved Son,
The Holy Ghost, the Comforter,
The Church doth worship and revere.

O Christ, Thou glorious King, we own
Thee to be God's eternal Son:
Thou, undertaking in our room,
Didst not abhor the Virgin's womb:
The pains of death o'ercome by Thee,
Made heaven to all believers free.
At God's right hand Thou hast Thy seat,
And in Thy Father's glory great:
And we believe the day 's decreed
When Thou shalt judge the quick and dead.

Promote, we pray, Thy servants' good,
Redeemed with Thy most precious blood;
Among Thy saints make us ascend
To glory that shall never end;

Thy people with salvation crown,
Bless those, O Lord, that are Thine own;
Govern Thy Church, and, Lord, advance
Forever Thine inheritance.

From day to day, O Lord, do we
Highly exalt and honor Thee;
Thy name we worship and adore
World without end for evermore:
Vouchsafe, O Lord, we humbly pray,
To keep us safe from sin this day.
O Lord, have mercy on us all;
Have mercy on us when we call;
Thy mercy, Lord, to us dispense,
According to our confidence:
Lord, we have put our trust in Thee,
Confounded let us never be.
      Amen.

 Miscellaneous.

Erhalt uns Herr, bei deinem Wort.

A CHILD'S SONG AGAINST THE TWO ARCH-ENEMIES OF CHRIST
AND HIS HOLY CHURCH,—THE POPE AND THE TURK.

(C. Winkworth, "Choral Book for England," No. 103.)

LORD, keep us steadfast in Thy Word;
Curb those who fain by craft or sword
Would wrest the kingdom from Thy Son,
And set at naught all He hath done.

Lord Jesus Christ, Thy power make known,
For Thou art Lord of lords alone;
Defend Thy Christendom, that we
May evermore sing praise to Thee.

O Comforter of priceless worth,
Send peace and unity on earth;
Support us in our final strife,
And lead us out of death to life.

Nun treiben wir den Pabst heraus.

A SONG FOR THE CHILDREN, WHEREWITH THEY CAST OUT
THE POPE IN MID-LENT.

(Christian Examiner, 1860, p. 244.)

WE drive the Pope with iron rod
From church of Christ and house of God,
Where he has murderously ruled,
And many precious souls befooled.

Pack off, begone, apostate son!
Thou scarlet bride of Babylon!
Thou art the Beast and Antichrist,
Whose lies have many a soul enticed.

Thy bulls and thy decretals lie
All sealed and hid from every eye,
That robbed the world in God's own name,
And put Christ's blood to open shame.

The Romish Dagon's lost his head;
The rightful Pope we take instead:
'Tis Christ, the Rock, God's only Son,
Whom His true Church is built upon.

High Priest o'er all is He, Lord Christ,
Who on the cross was sacrificed;
His blood flowed freely for our sin,
His wounds the true indulgence win.

The Church obeys His Word's behest;
Him God the Father doth invest;
The Head of Christendom is He:
Praised be His name eternally.

Now summer-time will soon appear;
Christ send us all a peaceful year!
Lord, save us from the Pope and Turk.
And finish all Thy blessed work!

Ein neues Lied wir heben an.

A SONG CONCERNING TWO CHRISTIAN MARTYRS BURNED AT BRUSSELS, IN 1523, BY THE SOPHISTS OF LOUVAIN.

(R. Massie, "Spiritual Songs," p. 40.)

By help of God I fain would tell
A new and wondrous story,
And sing a marvel that befell
To His great praise and glory.

At Brussels in the Netherlands
    He hath His banner lifted,
To show His wonders by the hands
    Of two youths, highly gifted
With rich and heavenly graces.

One of these youths was called John,
    And Henry was the other;
Rich in the grace of God was one,
    A Christian true his brother.
For God's dear Word they shed their blood,
    And from the world departed
Like bold and pious sons of God;
    Faithful and lionhearted,
They won the crown of martyrs.

The old Arch-fiend did them immure,
    To terrify them seeking;
They bade them God's dear Word abjure,
    And fain would stop their speaking.
From Louvain many Sophists came,
    Versed deeply in the schools,
And met together at the game;
    The Spirit made them fools,—
They could not but be losers.

Now sweet, now harsher tones they tried,
    In artifice abounding;
The youths did firm as rocks abide,
    The Sophists all confounding.
The enemy waxed fierce in hate,
    And for their life-blood thirsted;
He fumed and chafed that one so great
    Should by two babes be worsted,
And straightway sought to burn them.

Their monkish garb from them they take,
    And gown of ordination;
The youths a cheerful Amen spake,
    And showed no hesitation.
They thanked their God that by His aid
    They now had been denuded
Of Satan's mock and masquerade,
    Whereby he had deluded
The world with false pretences.

Thus by the power of grace they were
    True priests of God's own making,
Who offered up themselves e'en there,
    Christ's holy orders taking;

Dead to the world, they cast aside
　Hypocrisy's sour leaven,
That penitent and justified
　They might go clean to heaven,
And leave all monkish follies.

They then were told that they must read
　A note which was dictated;
They straightway wrote their faith and creed,
　And not one jot abated.
Now mark their heresy! "We must
　In God be firm believers;
In mortal men not put our trust,
　For they are all deceivers;"
For this they must be burned!

Two fires were lit; the youths were brought,
　But all were seized with wonder
To see them set the flames at naught,
　And stood as struck with thunder.
With joy they came in sight of all,
　And sang aloud God's praises;
The Sophists' courage waxed small
　Before such wondrous traces
Of God's almighty finger.

The scandal they repent, and would
    Right gladly gloss it over;
They dare not boast their deed of blood,
    But seek the stain to cover.
They feel the shame within their breast,
    And charge therewith each other;
But now the Spirit cannot rest,
    For Abel 'gainst his brother
Doth cry aloud for vengeance.

Their ashes never cease to cry,
    The fires are ever flaming,
Their dust throughout the world doth fly,
    Their murderers' shame proclaiming.
The voices which with cruel hands
    They put to silence living,
Are heard, though dead, throughout all lands
    Their testimony giving,
And loud hosannahs singing.

From lies to lies they still proceed,
    And feign forthwith a story
To color o'er the murderous deed;
    Their conscience pricks them sorely.

These saints of God e'en after death
    They slandered, and asserted
The youths had with their latest breath
    Confessed, and been converted,
Their heresy renouncing.

Then let them still go on and lie,
    They cannot win a blessing;
And let us thank God heartily,
    His Word again possessing.
Summer is even at our door,
    The winter now hath vanished,
The tender flowerets spring once more,
    And He, who winter banished,
Will send a happy summer.

INDEX OF FIRST GERMAN LINES.

	PAGE
Ach Gott vom Himmel sieh darein,	111
Aus tiefer Noth schrei ich zu dir,	144
Christ lag in Todesbanden,	50
Christ unser Herr zum Jordan ging,	140
Christum wir sollen loben schon,	41
Der du bist drei in Einigkeit,	73
Diess sind die heiligen zehn Gebot,	127
Ein feste Burg ist unser Gott,	78
Ein neues Lied wir heben an,	169
Erhalt uns Herr bei deinem Wort,	166
Es spricht der Unweisen Mund,	107
Es wolt uns Gott genädig sein,	124
Gelobet seist du, Jesu Christ,	42
Gott der Vater wohn uns bei,	74
Gott sei gelobet und gebenedeiet,	153
Herr Gott dich loben wir,	162
Jesaja, dem Propheten, das geschah,	161
Jesus Christus unser Heiland, der den Tod,	49
Jesus Christus unser Heiland, der von uns,	151
Komm Gott, Schöpfer, Heiliger Geist,	67
Komm heiliger Geist, Herre Gott,	56
Mensch willt du leben seliglich,	126
Mit Fried und Freud fahr ich dahin,	159
Mitten wir im Leben sind,	156

	PAGE
Nun bitten wir den Heiligen Geist, ...	70
Nun freut euch, lieben Christen gemein, . . .	116
Nun komm der Heiden heiland, ...	31
Nun treiben wir den Pabst heraus, ...	167
Sie ist mir lieb die werthe Magd, ...	76
Vater unser im Himmelreich, ...	133
Verleih uns Frieden gnädiglich, ...	139
Vom Himmel hoch da komm ich her, ...	36
Vom Himmel kam der Engel Schaar, ...	39
Was fürcht'st du Feind Herodes sehr, ...	47
Wär Gott nicht mit uns diese Zeit, ...	115
Wir glauben all an einen Gott, ...	131
Wohl dem der in Gottesfurcht steht, ...	122

INDEX OF FIRST ENGLISH LINES.

	PAGE
A castle is our God, a tower,	103
A fortress firm and steadfast rock,	94
A fortress firm is God our Lord,	80
A mighty fortress is our God,	96
A mountain fastness is our God,	82
A safe stronghold our God is still,	84, 86
A stronghold firm, a trusty shield,	91
A sure stronghold our God is He,	101
A tower of safety is our God,	89
A tower of strength our God doth stand,	98
All praise to Jesus' hallowed name,	42
Blest Comforter, come, Lord our God,	62
By help of God I fain would tell,	169
Christ who freed our souls from danger,	151
Come, Holy Ghost, come, Lord our God,	61
Come, Holy Ghost, Lord God, fulfil,	65
Come, Holy Ghost, rule thou within,	66
Come, Holy Spirit, God and Lord,	63
Come, Holy Spirite, most blessed Lorde,	59
Creator Spirit, holy Dove,	68
Dear Christian people, now rejoice,	116
Dear is to me the holy Maid,	76
From deep distress to Thee I pray,	148
From heaven above to earth I come,	36
God is our refuge in distress,	79, 105
God is our stronghold firm and sure,	99

INDEX OF FIRST ENGLISH LINES.

	PAGE
Had God not come, may Israel say,	. 115
Happy the man who feareth God,	. 122
In peace and joy I now depart, .	. 159
In the bonds of death He lay,	. 50
In the midst of life, behold, .	. 157
In these our days so perilous,	. 139
Jesus Christ to-day is risen, . . .	49
Look down, O Lord, from heaven behold, .	111
Lord God, thy praise we sing, .	163
Lord, keep us steadfast in Thy Word, .	. 166
May God be praised henceforth, .	. 153
Now crave we of the Holy Ghost,	71
Now praise we Christ, the holy one,	41
O thou Redeemer of our race, . . .	. 32
Our Father, thou in heaven above, . .	. 133
Our God, a tower of strength is He, . . .	87
Our God, He is a fortress tower, . .	. 93
Our God, our Father, with us stay, .	. 74
Out of the deep I cry to Thee, . . .	149
Out of the deeps of long distress, .	146
Out of the depth I cry to Thee, .	. 144
That men a godly life might live,	. 127
The mouth of fools doth God confess, . .	. 107
These things the seer Isaiah did befall,	. 161
Thou only God, the Three in One,	. 73
To Jordan came our Lord the Christ, .	140
To shepherds as they watched by night, . .	. 39
To us, O God, impart Thy grace, . .	. 124
We all believe in one true God, . .	. 131
We drive the Pope with iron rod, . . .	. 167
Why, Herod, unrelenting foe,	. 47
Wilt thou, O man, live happily, ...	. 126

www.ingramcontent.com/pod-product-compliance
Lightning Source LLC
Chambersburg PA
CBHW032154160426
43197CB00008B/916